S0-ECN-295

The Socioeconomic Approach To Status Measurement

(With a GUIDE To Occupational and Socioeconomic Status Scores)

The Socioeconomic Approach To Status Measurement

(With a GUIDE To Occupational and Socioeconomic Status Scores)

by

Charles B. Nam and Mary G. Powers

Cap and Gown Press
Houston

Cap and Gown Press, Inc.
Box 58825
Houston, Texas 77258
U.S.A.

Library of Congress Catalog Card Number: 82-73819

ISBN 0-88105-011-3 (Clothbound edition)

Printed in the United States of America

CONTENTS

Preface

Trends and differences in social status have long been recognized as critical elements in the structure and functioning of American social institutions. The mechanisms through which status influences other aspects of society and its relative importance have been debated for centuries. There have also been differences of opinion as to how status should be measured, although numerous status indexes and scales can be found in the literature.

Certainly, students of social stratification have identified significant elements of overall social status. Included among these are distinctions between prestige and socioeconomic status, as well as several indicators of each of those dimensions. It appears that more attention has been given to prestige than to socioeconomic status in recent social science research. This book is an attempt to redress the balance in social measurement by concentrating on socioeconomic indicators. More specifically, we have presented coverage of the socioeconomic indexes introduced as part of the Bureau of the Census program in 1960 and extended by the authors in the past several years.

Chapter 1 gives a summary review of the status measurement literature as a means of placing our own studies within an appropriate context. Chapter 2 traces the historical interest in socioeconomic measurement by the Bureau of the Census and shows the gradual evolution of census status measures over time. In Chapters 3 and 4, we have outlined procedures for the derivation of occupational status scores, multiple-item socioeconomic scores, and status consistency-inconsistency types, along with some examples of their uses. Further illustrative uses of these measures are found in Chapters 5 and 6, which include special analyses of sex and racial factors in status differences. Chapter 7 focuses on status dynamics over time and the important correlates of stability and change. Not the least vital part of the volume is the Appendix, which incorporates the variety of status scores and types which are available for research use in a broad range of situations, along with an outline of steps for applying them in research studies.

The effort expended here, while original in many respects, builds on the work of a number of persons and profits from the contributions of several people. In addition to those pioneers in census socioeconomic analysis, mentioned in Chapter 2, we are especially grateful to our former colleagues Paul Glick, Edward Stockwell, and the late Howard Brunsman, who made critical suggestions for the development of measures specified here, and to former students Nancy Curtis, Ruth Gindin, Joan Holmberg, John LaRocque, Ann Lencyk Pawliczko, and E. Walter Terrie, whose research papers and theses provided analyses which have been included in this book. We must also acknowledge previous research support from the National Science Foundation (Grant GSOC73-05786) through which some of the material reported here was developed. We are also indebted to E. Gartly Jaco, Editor of Cap and Gown Press, and his staff for helping us put this book together and making it available to the public.

The essential product which emerges, however, is ours for whatever utility it may bring to scientific and programmatic advancement. We hope that it will serve the reader well, and we will be grateful for any comments which might guide us in our continuing work in this area.

Charles B. Nam
Florida State University

Mary G. Powers
Fordham University

LIST OF TABLES AND FIGURES

Tables: Page:

Figures:

Chapter 1

Approaches to Status Measurement: An Overview

1
Approaches to Status Measurement: An Overview

There has been for some time a need for a scheme which would be useful in assessing status levels of individuals and groups for purposes of research and program planning. Measuring status is important for researchers of social stratification and for social scientists trying to link status to various behaviors. These measurements are also needed for program administrators who want to learn about the representativeness of their clientele and those in the business world who wish to describe their target populations in status terms.

Although at present there is no single generally accepted status classification scheme, social science researchers have produced a variety of indexes and scales. Most of these indexes and scales include occupation as a part of their measure, but other factors such as income, education, housing, and other variables figure prominently in a number of schemes.

This chapter provides an overview of the major approaches to status measurement by non-governmental employees, including those which rely primarily on occupational information and those which focus on other variables. Later chapters will deal with status measurement in the history of the U.S. Bureau of the Census and with two approaches which have been developed by the authors and their colleagues.

Occupation in Status Measurement

No one claims that occupation is the sole criterion of position within the stratification system in American society. Indeed, many early studies attempted to identify total social position in terms of several dimensions of community status, personal reputation, family background, education, occupation, income, and wealth (Warner and Lunt, 1947; Hollingshead, 1949). This sort of approach is not practicable on a national scale, however, where appraisal of an individual's status often must be made on the basis of relatively simple and visible indicators.

There has been substantial agreement among sociologists for some time that occupation is such an indicator. There has also accumulated considerable empirical and theoretical evidence of its validity as an index of social status.

Warner's early studies found that one's occupation showed the highest correlation with the prestige rank accorded his family in the local community (Warner, et al., 1949). More recently, Blau and Duncan (1949) and Caplow (1954) noted that in industrial societies occupation replaces other status attributes such as ancestry and religious or political office as a concise index of socioeconomic status.

Caplow's cogent explanation as to why occupation came to replace most other attributes as an index of status deserves special note. He suggests that the sheer increase in the size of social groups in contemporary society led to the substitution of formal organizations for less formal groupings. Large corporations and bureaucracies are characterized by anonymity and by defining responsibilities in terms of an office rather than an individual. As occupational specialization increased, the scope of each person's activity became less known to other persons, particularly to persons in other occupations. Thus one tends to respond to an occupational title rather than to individual qualifications.

It has been suggested (Moore, 1978) that as the occupational structure became more specialized and knowledge of attributes associated with specific occupations became more limited among the general public, the preference for the use of an objective measure of occupational status became more pronounced among social science researchers.

In addition, the increase in rationalization within society leads to the presumption that one's occupational position has been determined by a variety of rational criteria and therefore occupational position becomes an indicator of ability, character, training skills, and other traits.

Once occupation became accepted as in indicator of a broader status position, sociologists began to inquire as to the meaning of occupational status. On the one hand, it has been interpreted as being synonymous with prestige or position based on a subjective evaluation that individuals make of one another. On the other hand, it has been defined in terms of more objective criteria which include the educational level required for the occupation, the income associated with, and the degree of power which the occupation carries.

These different conceptualizations have resulted from different approaches to the study of occupational status. Historically, one can broadly categorize three major approaches: One measures occupational status in terms of the prestige accorded a sample of occupations by a sample of individual raters. The second uses objective data to estimate the rating that would be obtained by a prestige assessment. The third assigns a status score based on some form of objective measure alone, such as ranking the average educational and/or income levels of occupational groups.

Studies of Occupational Prestige: Early Efforts

The idea of measuring status by having individuals give their opinions about the social standing of specific occupations has existed for some time (Davies, 1952) and is still current today. Several major studies have made this approach popular, but one can trace back in time some of the less-frequently cited research which led to the more sophisticated approaches to which we will give major attention.

Many of the early efforts sampled students and teachers. In one of the earliest studies, a sample of 450 college and high school students and teachers were asked to rank 45 familiar occupations (Counts, 1925). The respondents consisted of six groups of students and teachers in Minnesota and in Connecticut. In general there tended to be agreement in the ranking of the 45 occupations among all six groups. There was strong agreement about the rankings given to occupations at the extreme ends of the scale. The hod-carrier, ditch-digger, physician and college professor were clearly defined occupations and there was more agreement as to their status than there was on insurance agent and farmer. Although a high level of agreement was found among the rankings, it appeared that such a sample was biased and the list of occupations was limited. Nonetheless, this and other pioneering efforts suggested that the general public could and did think of occupation in hierarchical terms.

In 1926 a method similar to Counts was used to rank 24 occupations by 609 students at North Carolina State College (Anderson, 1927-28). The respondents were basically rural boys and small town businessmen with very few sons of unskilled laborers included. The rankings of all 609 students agree rather closely, with only slight differences in the ranks assigned to the 24 occupations. The earlier study by Counts and this replication suggested that each occupation was accorded a fairly definite status in the minds of student raters. Based on their rankings six general classes of occupations were identified as follows:

1 - Professional groups
2 - Business occupations
3 - Skilled trades
4 - Recreational occupations
5 - Unskilled work
6 - "Man of leisure"

The "Man of Leisure" category was so vaguely defined that it was accorded many different positions. The other occupations were fairly similarly ranked by all of the samples, however.

A study by Wilkinson in 1929 attempted to discover how and why social distance varied between occupational groups by getting the reactions of a sample of 861 University of Southern California students to statements on a modification of the Bogardus Social Distance Scale. The sample included students from several different schools within the university — Liberal Arts, Education, Law, Dentistry, Religion and Commerce. In general, there was little "distance" shown towards the teacher, doctor and lawyer, but much more towards the hobo and fortune teller. It was obvious from this study that there was much less social distance towards occupations with relatively high status and/or prestige and more social distance felt towards occupations with little status and/or societal disapproval. Those occupations involving labor and menial service, such as day laborer, factory worker and servants, appeared to have a very definite "place" in society. For example, whereas 832 respondents would admit teachers to their club, only 190 would admit waiters. Again there was almost complete agreement about placing occupations such as teachers and "dope seller" at both ends of the scale and much more uncertainty about the positions of those in the middle such as movie star and insurance agent. The study demonstrated that the status of a given occupation was a fairly reliable index of how much social distance it would be accorded.

Students continued to be a favorite study group in the 1930's. A study by Lehman and Witty (1931) sampled youth between the ages of 8½ and 18½ and asked them to rank 26 occupations. Their findings were not unlike the earlier studies and showed that physicians were ranked on top of the list by both boys and girls and by practically every age level, but also showed that there were some very definite differences by sex with respect to ranking occupations such as the ministry. Girls tended to show greater respect for the clergy than adolescent boys. Girls also tended to give higher rankings to all kinds of educational endeavors than boys and more of them were apt to enter those fields. The Lehman and Witty study differed from Counts' research in that they asked their respondents to choose the three most respected occupations from a list of 200, whereas Counts asked his subjects to rank 45 occupations. Also Count's subjects were fewer and older and he took no account of age and sex differences. Nonetheless, the findings tend to agree generally with one another; for example, both revealed that the banker and physician were rated very highly.

G.W. Hartman (1934) asked 250 judges from various fields to arrange 25 occupations in a prestige hierarchy. His assumption was that persons confer prestige and reputation according to their social values. His method consisted of showing the interviewee cards containing the name of a single occupation and asking that they be put "in order of your admiration for the professions or vocations here given." The sample consisted of people from industrial towns and cities as well as from small villages. There was a great deal of consistency in the rankings given to occupations by respondents in all residential areas, small and large communities, and agricultural and industrial areas. All of the professions ranked near the top and labor near the bottom. Again physicians were uniformly placed first.

This study added a new dimension in that Hartman measured class consciousness or what he called "occupational insight" by comparing the rankings of an occupation by those in it with the rankings of others, and found little evidence of marked bias. Most respondents had a relatively precise notion of the place of each occupation within the hierarchy, and assigned their own job only a slightly higher position than the average one given to it. Of course, Hartman was again dealing with a relatively small number of occupations. Interest in the educational profession was again predominant and Hartman was particularly impressed with the hierarchical structure within the teaching profession: 5 of the 25 occupations were educational with college professors ranked first, school superintendents second, principals third, high school teachers fourth, and elementary school teachers fifth. Teachers ranked lowest among the professional occupations but relatively high when compared with all other occupations.

The consistency found among the results of these early studies resulted partly from the fact that the number of occupations to be ranked was relatively small and, for the most part, clearly defined. Even then it raised the question of whether the average individual is in a position to assign social status or prestige positions to any but a few well-defined occupations. The small number of occupations used in the earlier studies were not always the same occupations; hence by the mid-1930's there was a literature on occupational status based on relatively small samples of respondents ranking small numbers of occupations which often differed from one study to the next.

Mapheus Smith (1935), in his review of the earlier research, noted (1) the need for a rating technique which would objectify the distinction between occupations, (2) that any such rating scale had to include all occupations and every type of position within an occupational group, and (3) should result in a numerical value for each occupation and position within the occupational group. He realized it would be impractical to rate all occupations and positions but felt that a rating of 600 positions on a 100 point scale would be significant. His initial criticism of the studies made during the 1920's and 1930's was that there was no way of combining them into a single rank-order scale representative of occupational prestige in the country and he set out to construct such a scale. He asked 345 college undergraduates, high school seniors, and other high school students to rank 100 occupations. A numerical value was obtained for the prestige status of each occupation by combining (1) the rankings given each occupation when raters were asked to seat them according to their prestige rank at a dinner honoring a celebrity with (2) the rating these same people gave them on the basis of a 100 point scale. Again, occupations at the extreme ends of the scale stood out clearly in the minds of the raters compared to all others.

Smith divided the occupations into groups having similar rankings by rounding off the ratings received by the list of 100 occupations. The objective was to facilitate (1) defining horizontal groups or occupations that were alike with respect to status and (2) the understanding of horizontal and vertical mobility. Although he was one of the first to use a fairly large list of occupations, his own chief criticism of his work was that the larger classes of occupations in the society were not well represented in this prestige scale. Thus, it had limited value for the study of vertical and horizontal mobility.

In addition to interest in describing the social stratification system and the extent of mobility within it, a number of the early investigators were also concerned with the changing status of occupations and with determining whether external social conditions might affect the prestige status or rank of any occupations. One such study asked 2000 high school seniors to rank 40 occupations during 1928, 1932 and 1934 (Neitz, 1935). This was just before, at the height of, and after the worst of the "Great Depression." The author was particularly interested in seeing whether conditions resulting from the depression had changed the prestige ranking of any occupations. The 1928 rankings were made by students in Pennsylvania, the 1932 and 1934 rankings by students from three states but mostly high school seniors in Pennsylvania. Occupational rank was determined by adding the ranks given a particular occupation and then rearranging the occupations in the order of their rank value so that the lowest score was rank 1, the next lowest 2, and so forth. Over time, policeman, soldier, insurance agent, banker and bookkeeper increased most in prestige. Nietz attributed these increases to various specific causes: Policeman and soldier were accorded higher status later on, for example, because of fear of riots and revolutions during the depression period. The increased prestige of the insurance agent, he thought, may have been due to the fact that during the depression many people were subsisting on their insurance savings. He expected that the prestige accorded bankers would decrease, but when compared to Counts' earlier study, this occupation ranked two places higher. This may have been due to the fact that few bankers were jobless in the depression period. The occupations which decreased most in prestige or in social status included motorman, dry goods merchant, grocer, farmer and chauffeur. The dry goods merchants and grocers tended to close charge accounts during the depression and might have lost prestige as a result of this. The motorman's job was uncertain in those days since buses were replacing trolleys, and the plight of the farmer was a well-publicized one.

Comparing his study with that of Counts, Nietz noted that the greatest change in the top ten of the 40 occupations in his study amounted to only half a place in the ranking hierarchy, and only one occupation among the bottom ten, salesmen, changed as much as 3½ positions. Most change occurred among the middle 20 occupations, such as those mentioned above, and only four occupations increased in status by a changed ranking of five or more places. The electrician moved up eight places, the bookkeeper and locomotive engineer by five places each.

Other studies in the late 1930's and early 1940's also focused on occupational prestige, either by measuring the attitudes of professional students towards their own professions (Coutu, 1936) or asking samples of students to rate occupations according to multiple criteria on which they were thought to differ (Osgood and Stagner, 1941). Most of these produced about the same results as the studies summarized above.

In 1947 Counts study was replicated by Deeg and Patterson (1947) in an attempt to determine whether or not there had been any change in the social status rankings of occupations over the 21-year period between these studies. They suspected that the need for and productive value of defense jobs during the war years might have affected the prestige and social status of such occupations as coal miners, Army captains, and machinists who might have been expected to move up the social status scale. They ranked only 25 of the occupations on Counts' list. These represented the same range of occupations because they were chosen by deleting every other one on the Counts list and then adding three from widely separated points. A slight change was made by substituting truck driver for teamster. The instructions to the raters were worded exactly as were Counts'. Also, as in the Counts study, they listed the occupations alphabetically and gave a parenthetical description of the work involved. Their raters also bore a close resemblance to those used by Counts, except that they came from a single geographical locality.

Counts found, however, that there was little difference associated with raters from different localities. The Deeg and Patterson sample included: (1) University of Minnesota college freshmen, (2) juniors, seniors and graduate students in a psychology class at the same university, (3) seniors at Minneapolis Vocational high school, and (4) seniors at St. Paul's Academic high school. The results showed that only three occupations had been displaced by more than two ranks: Farmer dropped three places, traveling salesman dropped five places, and insurance agent moved up four places. Nietz had found similar changes in 1935. None of the occupations which changed were high-prestige occupations. Deg and Patterson concluded that the social status positions of occupations had changed very little and that the factors determining the relative prestige of occupations "continue to operate in a consistent manner".

As noted earlier, scholars on this topic continually felt the need to relate the results of the different studies. Clark (1948) ranked occupations according to prestige by comparing the results of the studies of Nietz, Smith, and Counts among whom were high rates of agreement. Clark noted that the prestige assigned any given occupation in the United States was somewhat stable over time and geographic area. He found a positive correlation of +.95 between the prestige rankings of Counts and Nietz. For his own purposes, Clark grouped the specific occupations ranked by Smith, Counts and Nietz into 17 groups. He found no disagreement about the bottom five or the top six occupations in the three studies. His interest was not in the prestige of occupations *per se*, but in the relationship between occupational prestige and psychoses. The value of his study, however, is in demonstrating the very high agreement obtained by combining the prestige rankings of each of the earlier studies and the high rank-order coefficient of correlation between income and prestige rankings.

Most of these early studies of occupational prestige assumed: (1) that the source of prestige of an occupation lay in the opinions of people rather than the characteristics of the occupation, and (2) that people could perceive and articulate the prestige levels.

Still other studies tended to confirm the findings of those cited. For example, Anderson's 1927 and 1934 rankings of 25 occupations according to social status and economic return showed that students related prestige very closely to economic return. The Bogardus social distance study of occupations, when turned into rankings, gave a picture similar to that found by Counts. Hartman's ranking of 25 occupations in 1934 confirmed the same picture as did the Osgood and Stagner general prestige rankings. Cattell (1942) compared the rankings of 26 occupations by a group of college students with the rankings of skilled and unskilled laborers and found essential agreement except for five occupations.

In most of these studies, occupations at the extreme ends of the scale were ranked with a very high degree of consistency. There was somewhat less agreement about those in the middle. This may have been due to a number of factors. First, new and/or unfamiliar occupations, occupations peculiar to a given region or area, and those with ambiguous standing such as salesmen, actor and insurance agent were usually placed in the middle. Second, the subjects in most of the studies tended to be college students, school teachers, and school children. There was basic agreement among them; however, teachers were usually more consistent than children and university students more so than skilled and unskilled workers. In effect, most of the studies showed that people could produce some sort of rank order of occupations when forced to reach some conclusion. They illustrate the early attempts to develop occupational prestige scales. Also they may serve as a basis for comparisons with the later NORC prestige studies and replications to assess the stability of occupational prestige over time.

Studies of Occupational Prestige: The Last 3½ Decades

The first sophisticated scale of occupational prestige was perhaps developed by the National Opinion Research Center (NORC) in 1947. In the Spring of 1947, the National Opinion Research Center sampled a cross-section of the American population to determine basic public attitudes towards occupations. In the fall of that year, Cecil North and Paul Hatt (1949) wrote a preliminary analysis of the data, and, hence, the scale is often referred to as the North-Hatt scale. That seminal study provided a starting point for much other research for the next three decades.

A list of 100 occupations was constructed which was presumed to be representative of the entire range of legitimate occupations in the United States. In an attempt to keep the number within practical limits, the list was reduced to 78 occupations, eliminating "women's occupations" such as private secretary, dressmaker, trained nurse, etc. Before going into the field, however, an additional nine occupations were added to the list by the President's Scientific Advisory Board and three more by NORC, so that the final list included 90 occupations.

The sample of 2900 people was asked to evaluate each of the 90 occupations according to their "own personal opinion of the general standing" of a person engaged in that occupation. A five point scale was provided with ratings of (1) excellent standing, (2) good standing, (3) average standing, (4) somewhat below average standing, (5) poor standing. Also an "x-rating" which meant "I don't know where to place that one" was shown to the respondents. On the basis of the overall replies, the responses were scored 100, 80, 60, 40 and 20 respectively. The "don't know" responses were counted but were not assigned any particular value and were not entered into the basic computation of the score. The prestige rating for each of the 90 occupations was calculated by taking the mean scores assigned to the occupation by the sample. The result was a scale ranging from 96 for Supreme Court Justice to 33 for shoe shiner. The occupations were then rearranged and ranked from 1 through 90 et al. (Reiss, 1961).

As with earlier research it was found that people tended to rank their own jobs and those like their own jobs somewhat higher than the average evaluation of those positions. The characteristic which appeared to be associated with a high occupational prestige ranking included highly specialized training and a considerable degree of responsibility for public welfare. The professions ranked highest, although age was found to make some difference in the ranking of occupations. For example, "bartender" received its highest rating from those in the 21 to 39 year old age group. Government offices were rated highest, with the professions as a whole coming in second. Among the professions, which accounted for about one-third of the 90 occupations listed, scores ranged from 93 for physician down to 52 for night club singer. The highest average ranking within the professions was given to the eight scientific occupations which, with the exception of economist, consistently ranked above the average score for professional and semi-professional work. The six nonfarm laboring jobs listed ranked lowest. People from all sections of the country were in marked agreement in their evaluation of most occupations. There were some consistent regional differences: Judges, psychologists, sociologists, economists and bartenders ranked relatively highest in the Northeast, and bookkeepers were ranked highest in the South where scientists and lawyers were ranked lowest. Priests were ranked highest in the Northeast and lowest in the Midwest.

Another innovation in this study was that respondents were asked *why* they rated occupations as they did. Specifically, they were asked to name the "one main thing"about the jobs they rated as excellent that gave them that standing. There was no predominant answer, and, in fact, no majority response. About 60 % of the responses were equally divided among answers such as "the job pays well", "it has social prestige", "it required a lot of education or hard work," "it performs a service to humanity" and/or "it's essential". Responses relating to income and education associated with the job were most frequently mentioned. Low income respondents most often mentioned financial reward as most important to the status of an occupation. It has been suggested that similarity in ratings but the apparent lack of agreement on what constitutes an "occupational standing" implies either that people have a single image of occupation to which they respond intuitively or that various criteria for judgment are highly interrelated (Svalastoga, 1965).

The NORC study is a landmark study for a number of reasons. It included a sizable number of occupations and, more important, it included a large enough sample of respondents so that some attention could be paid to the effects of age, educational level, and other characteristics on rankings. Indeed, although there was a fairly high consistency of response, there were some differences. For example, professional occupations, particularly the scientific jobs, were ranked higher by the college-educated than by all others. Those who completed no more than eight grades tended to rank skilled jobs, such as carpenter, and operative work, such as railroad conductor, higher than did others. On the other hand, the study contained some of the usual biases. As noted, one-third of all the occupations listed were professional jobs, a high proportion compared to the number in the total population, reflecting perhaps the biases of professional social scientists. Another point to be noted about this study is that the scientific jobs which were ranked so high were unfamiliar to many people. "Nuclear Physicists" were singled out to be defined by respondents in an attempt to infer how many people might have evaluated an occupation without being able to define it. Only three per cent of the respondents were able to give a completely correct definition of nuclear physicists and 18 per cent a partially correct one.

Although the NORC study proved to be a breakthrough in this kind of research, some smaller scale studies continued to be conducted throughout the 1940's. For example, in 1948, Welch (1950) surveyed 500 students at Indiana State Teachers College to see whether the ranking of Teachers College students differed from those of other students. The same occupations were ranked as were ranked in the Deeg and Patterson study, except that "high school teacher" was added to the list of occupations. When compared, a positive rank order correlation of .983 was found between the two studies. The entire group of raters generally grouped occupations into the conventional classification of professional, semi-professional, skilled, etc. and, as Welch noted "they have crystallized viewpoints".

Although the work summarized thus far was done in the United States, some valuable and relevant work on the status of occupation was being done in other countries, notably Britain, and some comparative research was also found. In England in 1949, the Hall-Jones study (1950) attempted to distinguish occupations according to prestige and to group them on the basis of similar prestige levels. The rationale behind that study was simply stated:

> If we are to trace changes in social class by changes in occupation, a preliminary examination of the social grading of occupations is essential.

The authors were involved in the Nuffield Foundation studies to discover the factors responsible for social class differences and social mobility in England and Wales. They intended to group people accordingly to occupation and wanted tests of whether their classification of occupations was consistent with popular opinion. They sampled 343 respondents in a pilot study and 1,056 subjects in their larger general study. The respondents were mostly middle-class persons from adult education classes, Civil Service associations, union members, local government association members, and life insurance workers. They were asked to group 30 occupations into seven prestige classes, and then to arrange the prestige classes "in social grade order relative to each other." When the results were tabulated and the occupations grouped into classes, there appeared to be a clear prestige division between those occupations in classes 5 and 6 and those in classes 2 and 3. The differences between 3 and 4 and 4 and 5 were not so clearly defined, however. As in the earlier research in the United States, they, too, found few differences among the raters from different groups, although those in professional and administrative posts seemed more consistent in their judgment than those in manual and routine clerical occupations. They found that people did tend to place occupations into groups which were very much like the classification they hoped to use in the Nuffield Foundation studies.

Somewhat later, Inkeles and Rossi (1956) made a comparison of the prestige accorded comparable occupations in six industrial countries: United States, Great Britain, New Zealand, Japan, the U.S.S.R., and Germany. High correlations were found among prestige rankings in the various countries and they suggested that occupations are ranked according to prestige in a relatively standard hierarchy regardless of cultural differences among the six nations.

Despite the high degree of consistency among scales, the legitimacy of any scale of occupational prestige was questioned by Davies (1952) more than a quarter of a century ago. He noted in his critique that the same occupation was ranked somewhat differently in different regions of the same society and sometimes varied with the social status of the informant. Davies also felt that there were different types of recognition of occupational prestige because people rated higher those occupations similar to their own. He also questioned the singleness of a hierarchy of differently placed occupations. This last criticism is one which has concerned social scientists because, when asked to rank occupations relative to one another, research subjects are forced to place in a hierarchical structure occupations which seem to be on the same group level when a point score rating system is used.

This difficulty with occupational prestige measures was discussed by Hatt (1950). He also questioned whether the measure of occupational prestige developed by them could be viewed as a single continuum and whether such dissimilar occupations as airline pilot, artist, factory owner, and sociologist could be evaluated on the same continuum by respondents. He used the Guttman scaling technique on three different subsets of NORC items and found that the respondents were, in fact, using several ranking systems. On reexamining the scores, he divided them into subgroups which seemed to scale on a single continuum and developed the idea of parallel status ladders which he called "situses." Hatt identified eight separate situses: Political, professional, business, recreation and aesthetics, agricultural, manual work, military, and service occupations. His research suggested that statuses within a single situs might easily be compared but comparisons across situs lines resulted in ambiguous findings. This development of the concept of situs was an important addition and was used in the 1963 retest of the NORC occupational prestige scores to analyze changes in prestige for homogeneous groupings of occupations. Beyond that, however, it has not been widely used.

The NORC scores have been a major contribution to the study of occupational prestige, particularly after a 1963 replication demonstrated the stability of the ratings over time. In spite of the conceptional and methodological difficulties and the limited scope of the scale, it continues to be widely used. The most recent adaptation of the NORC prestige scores appears in a doctoral dissertation by Siegel (1971). He has derived a new set of occupational prestige scores by combining the occupational prestige ratings collected in three separate studies, the NORC 1963 replication and two other studies conducted in 1964 and 1965 by Siegel and his colleagues. Regression techniques were used to link the scores. These were then developed into a set of scores for detailed occupational categories as shown in the 1960 Census labor force.

The occupational prestige ratings collected in several surveys used by Siegel were based on different samples, different lists of occupations, and on somewhat different methodologies, but all were combined into a single list. For example, in the Hodge, Siegel and Rossi study (1964) an area probability sample of 923 respondents was asked to estimate the social standing of 203 occupational titles by placing a card with an occupation typed on it on a large piece of cardboard containing nine boxes on a ladder. The boxes were numbered one through nine, and the first, fifth and ninth boxes labelled bottom, middle and top, respectively. The respondents were also asked to rate the occupation of their family's chief earner. The three subsets of occupations included in the list of 203 were: (1)occupations taken from the census lists; (2) those which matched the post-enumeration study of scientific and technical manpower conducted by NORC and (3) occupations which were missing from most of the previous subsets, such as political jobs. Occupations were scored in terms of the boxes into which they had been sorted. The nine intervals on the ladder were scored from bottom to top as 0, 12.5, 25, 37.5, etc. and the score received by an occupation is the average score of the boxes into which it was scored. Theoretically this might range from 0 to 100. In 1965, a supplementary survey of occupational prestige was conducted in which 153 occupational titles were rated in exactly the same manner as in the Hodge, Siegel, Rossi survey. These were occupations which were chosen to be used in conjunction with the Hodge, Siegel, Rossi survey and the NORC replications to provide the basis for assigning prestige scores to each of the detailed occupational categories in the 1960 Census classification scheme. There were different versions of the supplementary study and a sample of approximately 500 persons was asked to rate occupations on each supplement.

Because the ratings for the NORC replication and for the Hodge, Siegel, Rossi study were scaled differently, the mean ratings of occupations in the replication and in the supplementary study had to be transformed into prestige scores in the metric of the Hodge, Siegel, Rossi study. In all the studies combined, over 600 occupational titles were used, only 412 of which were distinct titles, the others having been rated more than once. This overlap of identically worded titles permitted the transformations to occur. The overlapping titles were used to establish four regression lines predicting the prestige scores in the Hodge, Siegel, Rossi study from the mean rating each title received in each of the other studies. There were 32 titles identically worded in the 1963 NORC replication and the Hodge, Siegel, Rossi study, and 49 titles common to both the Hodge, Siegel and Rossi study and each of the supplements. These were used to establish the regressions. The regression equations were then used to provide what Siegel called "prestige scores in uniform metric" for all of the titles not rated in the Hodge, Siegel, Rossi study. The scores shown for titles rated in the Hodge, Siegel, Rossi study were the prestige scores they actually received in that study. Prestige scores were then assigned to each of the detailed occupational titles shown in the 1960 Census of Population. A prestige score was also calculated for each major occupational group by getting a weighted average of the scores for detailed occupations which constituted the major group. The weights were provided by the distribution of the 1960 experienced civilian labor force and, ultimately, decile scores were derived for each occupation which represented groups of incumbents in the occupation which were of approximately equal size at the time of the 1960 Census.

Perhaps because of the recency of its development and the complicated nature of the statistical procedures, the Siegel prestige scores in uniform metric have not been as widely used as the original NORC or its 1963 replication. The set of scores provided by Siegel has an advantage over the earlier NORC work insofar as it provides a score for each of the detailed occupational categories listed in the census. However, it does not appear to have overcome any of the difficulties inherent in the earlier studies. Indeed, the errors made might even be compounded because so many of the scores were artificially derived from mathematical estimates rather than from direct ratings by respondents.

Linking Prestige and Socioeconomic Criteria

Measuring status based on popular judgments about occupations alone has been dissatisfying to many students of the field. The dissatisfaction stems from lack of firm knowledge about what are the sources of popular ratings as well as indications that there is some disparity between prestige and socioeconomic criteria of status determination.

One of the early social class studies focused on the relationship of the two approaches. Warner (1949) classified the residents of the community he studied both by reputation (what he called Evaluated Participation) and socioeconomic indicators (what he called Status Characteristics). The reputational approach did not rely on occupation alone but instead required community members to rate each other by a number of criteria. An Index of Status Characteristics (ISC) was a measurement based on a weighted combination of occupation, source of income, house type, and dwelling area. While both EP and ISC were highly correlated empirically, there were some differences. Warner saw the ISC as being a shorthand way of determining Evaluated Participation, which he felt was the crux of social status determination.

One of Warner's earlier colleagues, August Hollingshead (1949), attempted to simplify the reputational approach by having respondents in one of Warner's communities sort families on several criteria and combining the results into class categories. In an effort to use more objective variables for status placement, Hollingshead then developed a set of classes based on residential, occupational, and educational scales. Each of these had fixed categories and, when combined with "judged class position," a composite index was created. Ultimately the judgment item was dropped, producing a three-factor Index of Social Position. Still later, a two-factor Index was employed based on occupation and education, variables for which objective data were more readily available.

Later Duncan (1963) attempted to bridge the prestige-socioeconomic gap by producing his Socioeconomic Index for All Occupations. Using education and income to classify occupations according to socioeconomic levels, Duncan utilized this information to assign scores to a detailed list of occupations. His logic was essentially that suggested by Hatt much earlier: If education is an indicator of the prerequisite required for an occupation and income is a measure of the reward that society will bestow on an occupation, then occupation may be viewed as an intervening activity between these two variables and hence a good single indicator of status. A multidimensional scale was developed by using the education and income characteristics for each occupation contained in the 1950 Census. The income and educational levels of each occupation were calculated by computing the proportion of its incumbents found toward the "upper end" of the income and education distribution for the total male labor force. The upper end of education and income was defined as (1) the per cent in each occupation with a high school education and (2) the percent reporting incomes of $3500 or more. Age-specific education and income patterns for each occupation were incorporated as weights with indirect standardization used to obtain age-adjusted indicators for income and education. As in the earlier studies, the analysis was limited to the male labor force.

The Duncan "socioeconomic index of occupations" incorporated the prestige dimension of occupational status by using multiple regression analyses to arrive at estimates of prestige based on the 45 occupations in the original NORC study which precisely matched census categories. An estimate of the prestige of occupations was based on the linear multiple regression of the per cent with "excellent" or "good" prestige ratings on the average income and education of the 45 occupational categories which were comparable in the 1947 NORC study and the 1950 Census titles. Using the regression weights resulting from the calculation, Duncan assigned all of the 1950 Census occupations a score ranging from 0 to 96.

Duncan's index has become a widely used measure and has provided new direction in the measurement of occupational status. Nonetheless, it has been the subject of considerable criticism, much of which centers around his methodology and use of the 1947 NORC prestige scores. The following quotation is typical of such criticism:

> Regression and correlation techniques are peculiarly sensitive to the characteristics of the sample upon which they are based, and given the well known bias in the titles represented in the NORC study, one must question the reliability of any results derived from a sub-sample of them. If we regard Duncan's 45 titles as a sample of the 452 distinct census detailed occupational categories, we find the major occupational groups "professional, technical and kindred workers" and "service workers, except private household" are grossly over-represented while "operative and kindred workers" and "laborers" are grossly under represented (Siegel, 1971).

Although the use of occupation to measure social standing has been viewed positively in terms of bringing objectivity to the study of stratification, it has also been suggested that Duncan cancelled out some of the objectivity by ranking occupational standing according to the subjective evaluation suggested by the NORC prestige scores (Haug and Sussman, 1968).

In essence, the Duncan scores are an approximation of the ratings occupations would have received in the NORC study of 1947 if the raters had been asked to rate them, knew the amount of education an occupation required and the income accruing to it. The basis for this rationale is the high correlation between income and education and the NORC subjective ratings for the 45 occupations used to predict the other scores. In fact, Duncan (1963) himself noted that the index does not predict the prestige ratings that would have occurred if the NORC study was replicated to include additional occupations because this larger number of occupations would be much less known to the public than the original set. More important, however, is the question to what extent an understanding of the objective characteristics of an occupation, notably education and income, provides the basis for a prestige rating. Certainly knowledge about the educational and income levels of occupations would enter into judgement of its prestige value but there is considerable evidence to suggest that factors other than such knowledge also enter into the ranking.

In spite of the criticism and the shortcomings, the Duncan scores continue to enjoy widespread use and his research clearly demonstrates the relationship between the status level of an occupation and the education and income characteristics associated with that occupation. Revised and updated versions have been prepared (Stevens and Featherman, 1980; Featherman and Stevens, 1982).

The Socioeconomic Approach to Status Measurement

Researchers favoring the prestige approach to measuring occupational status have argued that it is prestige or perception of status we are usually interested in and a "pure prestige" approach is thus preferable. Others have argued that the difficulty of measuring prestige requires that we use objective indicators to assess prestige. Still others acknowledge a distinction between prestige and socioeconomic status and regard prestige scores as "error-prone" estimates of the socioeconomic attributes of occupations (Featherman and Hauser, 1976). They believe Duncan's scores are basically socioeconomic in nature, even though they are anchored to prestige ratings.

This controversy seems to ignore the advantage of the use of objective indicators for direct measurement of socioeconomic status without any reference to prestige. For many analytical uses, a measure of life chances or objective status conditions, is wanted, and this criterion for valuing occupation and constructing composite indexes leads to pure socioeconomic criteria.

A few non-governmental explorations involving the purely socioeconomic approach to status measurement can be cited here. They incorporate various items which are believed to reflect objective conditions of socioeconomic status.

Perhaps the earliest example of this approach was that of Blishen (1958) who arranged occupations in the Canadian census according to income and years of schooling. The average of each variable for each occupation was determined and standard scores of the two measures computed. These standard scores were then combined to denote an occupation's rank in the hierarchy. An arbitrary grouping of occupations produced seven "classes".

Bogue (1969) developed what he called an Index of Socioeconomic Achievement (SEA) which combines income and education associated with an occupation. Operationally, it requires that (1) income *expected* for an occupation on the basis of education alone be calculated, (2) *actual* income that is received be calculated, (3) the two averaged to arrive at a combined index, (4) if data are collected for several different dates, the data converted to "constant dollars" by adjusting for purchasing power, and (5) the result converted to an index number by dividing the average obtained by $20,000 and multiplying the result by 100. Mean income is used where averages are needed. The data are further controlled by age-standardization.

In an earlier study, Bogue (1962) introduced a socioeconomic score which was also based on education and income but using different procedures. (1) The median and first and third quartiles (Q_1, Q_2, Q_3) of educational attainment for each occupation were calculated. (2) The operation was repeated for quartiles of income for each occupation. (3) An index was developed for each variable (education and income) according to the formula $1/5\,(2Q_1 + Q_2 + 2Q_3)$, which accounted for the shape of the distribution. (4) Coefficients for weighting each index were based on Hagood's first-factor loading technique, adjusted so that a zero for each coefficient will yield a zero index and the average weighted index for all occupations equals 100.

Blau and Duncan (1967), although working extensively with Duncan's prestige-linked socioeconomic scores, also rank ordered 17 occupational groups according to their combined median income and education, and used this information to examine the flow of manpower or gross upward or downward mobility.

Hollingshead's Three-Factor and Two-Factor Indexes have already been mentioned. Although Hollingshead initially experimented with prestige-related indexes, he reverted to status indicators which were purely socioeconomic in nature.

Numerous other variations in socioeconomic status measurement can be found in the research literature. Individual researchers have often found existing measures inadequate for their purposes, either because requisite data were lacking or the conceptual basis, or calculating procedures, lacked appeal. At times, simple numerical measures of education (or of income) have been developed which incorporate a variety of indicators. In the well-known Indianapolis Fertility Study, Kiser and Whelpton (1949) classified the fertility of their respondents by a multiple-item SES score which included measures of husband's average annual earnings since marriage, net worth, shelter rent at interview, husband's longest occupational class since marriage, purchase price of automobile, education of husband, education of wife, and rating of the household on Chapin's Social Status Scale (a broader social participation measure).

Some of the most significant work on socioeconomic status measurement has been conducted by government employees, especially those at the Census Bureau. Chapter 2 provides an historical perspective of these efforts, and Chapters 3 and 4 elaborate socioeconomic measurement developed by the authors which are widely applicable and easy to use.

REFERENCES

Anderson, W.A. 1927-28. Occupational Attitudes and Choices of a Group of College Men, 1 and 2." *Social Forces* 6: 278-283 and 467-473.

Blau, Peter M. and Otis D. Duncan. 1967. *The American Occupational Structure.* New York: John Wiley.

Blishen, Bernard R. 1958. "The Construction and Use of an Occupational Class Scale." *Canadian Journal of Economics and Political Science* 24: 519-531.

Bogue, Donald J. 1962. *Skid Row in American Cities.* Chicago: Community and Family Study Center.

Bogue, Donald J. 1969. *Principles of Demography.* New York: John Wiley.

Caplow, Theodore. 1954. *The Sociology of Work.* Minneapolis: University of Minnesota Press.

Cattell, Raymond B. 1942. "The Concept of Social Status." *Journal of Social Psychology* 15: 293-308.

Clark, Robert E. 1948. "The Relationship of Schizophrenia to Occupational Income and Prestige." *American Sociological Review* 3: 325-330.

Counts, George. 1925. "The Social Status of Occupations." *The School Review* 33: 16-27.

Coutu, Walter. 1936. "The Relative Prestige of 20 Professions as Judged by Three Groups of Professional Students." *Social Forces* 14: 522-529.

Davies, A.F. 1952. "Prestige of Occupations." *British Journal of Sociology* 3: 134-147.

Deeg, M.E. and D.G. Patterson. 1947. "Changes in Social Status of Occupations." *Occupations* 25: 205-208.

Duncan, Otis D. 1961. "A Socioeconomic Index for All Occupations." In A.J. Reiss, *et al. Occupations and Social Status.* New York: Free Press.

Featherman, David L. and Gillian Stevens. 1982. "A Revised Socioeconomic Index of Occupational Status: Application in Analysis of Sex Differences in Attainment." In Mary G. Powers, ed. *Measures of Socioeconomic Status: Current Issues.* Boulder, CO: Westview Press.

Featherman, David L. and Robert M. Hauser. 1976. "Prestige or Socioeconomic Scales in the Study of Occupational Achievement?" *Sociological Methods and Research* 4: 402-422.

Hall, John and Caradog B. Jones. 1950. "Social Grading of Occupations." *British Journal of Sociology* 1: 31-55.

Hartman, G.W. 1934. "The Prestige of Occupations." *Personnel Journal* 13: 144-152.

Hatt, Paul K. 1950. "Occupations and Social Stratification." *American Journal of Sociology* 55: 533-543.

Haug, Marie and Marvin B. Sussman. 1968. "Social Class Measurement 2—The Case of the Duncan Set. Unpublished paper presented at the American Sociological Association meeting in Boston.

Hodge, Robert W., Paul M. Siegel and Peter H. Rossi. 1964. "Occupational Prestige in the United States: 1925-1963." *American Journal of Sociology* 70: 286-302.

Inkeles, Alex and Peter H. Rossi. 1956. "National Comparisons of Occupational Prestige." *American Journal of Sociology* 61: 329-339.

Hollingshead, August B. 1949. *Elmtown's Youth.* New York: John Wiley.

Kiser, Clyde V. and P.K. Whelpton. 1949. "Social and Psychological Factors Affecting Fertility: IX. Fertility Planning and Fertility Rates by Socioeconomic Status." *Milbank Memorial Fund Quarterly* 27: 188-244.

Lehman, H.C. and Paul A. Witty. 1931. "Further Study of the Social Status of Occupations." *Journal of Educational Sociology* 5: 101-112.

Moore, Wilbert A. 1978. Occupational Prestige and Social Inequality. Presented at American Sociological Association meeting in Boston.

Nietz, J.A. 1935. "The Depression and the Social Status of Occupations." *Elementary School Journal* 35: 454-461.

North, C.C. and Paul K. Hatt. 1947. "Jobs and Occupations: A Popular Evaluation." *Opinion News* 9: 3-13.

Osgood, C.E. and R. Stagner. 1941. "Analysis of the Prestige Frame of Reference by a Gradient Technique." *Journal of Applied Psychology* 25: 275-290.

Siegel, Paul M. 1971. Prestige in the American Occupational Structure. Unpublished doctoral dissertation, University of Chicago.

Smith, Mapheus. 1935. "Proposal for Making a Scale of Occupational Status." *Sociol- and Social Research* 20: 40-49.

Stevens, Gillian and David L. Featherman. 1980. A Revised Socioeconomic Index of Occupational Status. CDE Working Paper #79-48, University of Wisconsin-Madison.

Svalastoga, Kaare H. 1965. *Social Differentiation.* McKay Publishers.

Warner, W. Lloyd,Marchia Meeker and Kenneth Eells. 1949. *Social Class in America: The Evaluation of Status.* Chicago: Science Research Associates.

Warner, W. Lloyd and P.S. Lunt. 1947. *The Status System of a Modern Community.* New Haven, CT: Yale University Press.

Welch, M.K. 1950. "The Ranking of Occupations on the Basis of Social Status." *Occupations* 27: 237-241.

Wilkinson, Forrest. 1929. "Social Distance between Occupations." *Sociology and Social Research* 13: 234-244.

2
Census Socioeconomic Measures: Historical Perspective

The importance of status indicators in characterizing American society is well reflected in the history of the United States census. In this chapter we will attempt to answer the following questions about this historical development: When and how was occupational measurement introduced into the census? In what form did occupational classifications first appear? How has the occupational structure changed over time? When were occupations first viewed as status indicators? How did Alba Edwards construct his famous occupational status scheme? What other status related variables have been included in decennial censuses?

Occupations and the Founding Fathers

It has been said that the United States was the first country to provide for representative government at the time the nation was founded. Article I, Section 2 of the American Constitution specifies that

> Representatives and direct taxes shall be apportioned among the several States which may be included within this Union, according to their respective numbers, which shall be determined by adding to the whole number of free persons, including those bound to service for a term of years, and excluding Indians not taxed, three-fifths of all other persons. The actual enumeration shall be made within three years after the first meeting of the Congress of the United States, and within every subsequent term of ten years, in such manner as they shall by law direct (Rossiter, 1909).

The census was regarded by many as the basis for much more than apportioning the House of Representatives, however. Debates surrounding the establishment of the census and its procedures reflected a substantial feeling that the society should be guided by systematic planning and that knowledge of the social composition of the population was critical toward that end.

In the Federalist papers, a series of essays written in the late 1780's in support of the Constitution, the argument was made that political representatives needed to know about the kinds of people and lands they represented. Although the number of representatives in government must necessarily be limited, the essayist argued, it was possible to obtain local information through a variety of means (Hamilton et al., 1937).

James Madison, one of the authors of the Federalist papers and a framer of the Constitution, was a leading spokesman for the broader purpose of the census. When the first Congress was in session in 1789, a committee with members from every State prepared a bill outlining the provisions of the population enumeration to be taken for the first time in the decennial year following. In the debates on the bill, Madison pointed to the census as a prime basis for gathering the necessary information for governance. He proposed that information be collected on "the description of the several classes in which the community is divided" in order "to make a proper provision for the agricultural, commercial, and manufacturing interest." He remarked, furthermore, that "If the plan was pursued in taking every future census, it would give them an opportunity of marking the progress of the society, and distinguishing the growth of every interest (Gales, 1834,1077).

While Madison's ideas about occupational information in the census gained many supporters, they also found a number of opponents. Congressman Livermore complained that the proposal was "too extensive to be carried into operation, and divided the people into classes too minute to be readily ascertained." Moreover, he said, "Many inhabitants of New Hampshire pursued two, three, or four occupations, but which was the principal one depended upon the season of the year or some other adventurous circumstance." Public reaction to the inquiry was also a consideration, since "they could suspect that Government was too particular, in order to learn their ability to bear the burden of direct or other taxes" (Gales, 1834, 1108).

Arguments against elaborating the census schedule were reinforced by general agreement that taking the enumeration was a time-consuming operation that should not last longer than nine months (Rossiter, 1909, 43). Madison's provision for including occupations was carried in the House but defeated in the Senate, and the first census was a brief one which covered the categories "Free white males under 16," "Free white males above 16," "White females," "Free blacks," and "Slaves." However, such was the variability in schedule formats from area to area, and the latitude given marshals who colleted the 1790 census data, that the inquiries in two communities within Pennsylvania incorporated a question on occupation of heads of families. Although this was apparently to provide the basis for a city directory, it also resulted in the first occupational statistics for the new country (Rossiter, 1909, 142)

Madison's efforts to add officially an item on occupation to the first census had failed but did influence the collection of such information in a few places. In addition, the arguments he presented were carried forth by others. His views were shared by Thomas Jefferson who, just prior to the second census in 1800, presented a Memorial of the American Philosophical Society to the Senate and House of Representatives on more minute census returns (Padover, 1943). The Society, of which he was then President, wished to see the census ascertain "sundry facts highly interesting and important." Among these items further detailing the census would be more age categories "from whence may be calculated the ordinary duration of life in these States," citizenship, and data on occupations. Regarding the latter, he wrote:

> In order to ascertain more completely the causes which influence life and health, and to furnish a curious and useful document of the distribution of society in these States, and of the conditions and vocations of our fellow citizens, they propose that still another table shall be formed, specifying, in different columns, the number of free male inhabitants of all ages engaged in business, under the following or such other descriptions as the greater wisdom of the Legislature shall approve, to wit: 1. Men of the learned professions, including clergymen, lawyers, physicians, those employed in the fine arts, teachers and scribes, in general. 2. Merchants and traders, including bankers, insurers, brokers and dealers of every kind. 3. Mariners. 4. Handy craftsmen. 5. Labourers in agriculture. 6. Labourers of other descriptions. 7. Domestic servants. 8. Paupers. 9. Persons of no particular calling living on their income: care being to be taken, that every person be noted but once in this table, and that under the description to which he principally belongs.

At about the same time that Jefferson presented his memorial, Timothy Dwight signed one on behalf of the Connecticut Academy of Arts and Sciences in which it was recommended that the next census comprehend "the number of persons in each of the handicraft occupations; the number of merchants, cultivators of land, and professional men, distinguishing their professions" (Wright 1900). It was reported that these memorials reached the Senate and were referred to the committee which had responsibility for outlining the census content and procedures. But there is no indication that they received serious consideration and the recommendations on occupation were not adopted.

More often than not, Congressional bills which find their way into law may be submitted, declined, revised, and reconsidered one or more times before being accepted. The proposal for incorporating an item on occupations in the census met this fate several times before becoming part of the Census of 1820. Yet, the philosophy of some of the Founding Fathers had laid the groundwork for a broader view of the census as a social inventory of the nation.

Census Occupational Classifications Over Time

The particular categories of occupation specified at each census date reflect the social composition of the nation at the time. The increasing division of labor in American society can thus partly be observed by noting the occupational classifications used at each census.

Returns for the Census of 1790 from Southwark and parts of Philadelphia for heads of households in these largely urban areas showed five major occupational groupings — agricultural pursuits, professional service, domestic and personal service, trade and transportation, and manufacturing and mechanical pursuits. By far the largest numbers in Philadelphia were recorded as merchants and dealers, but relatively substantial numbers were identified as laborers, tailors, shoemakers, house carpenters, and inn and tavern keepers, occupations which reflected a growing city frequented by transients (Table 2-1). In Southwark, a coastal suburb, the relatively large number of laborers was complemented by a considerable count of sea captains, mariners, and mates (Rossiter, 1909, 142).

Table 2-1. Heads of Families in the Middle and Southern Districts of Philadelphia, and in Southwark, Classified According to Occupation: 1790

Occupation:	**Middle and southern districts of Philadelphia**	**Southwark**
All heads of families	3,434	970
Returned with occupation	2,758	827
Agricultural pursuits	15	3
Professional service	220	35
Artists	2	1
Attorneys at law	25	2
Clergymen	11	4
Doctors of physics, surgeons, dentists, etc.	27	4
Officials (government)	79	10
Schoolmasters and professors	71	14
All other professional services	5	--
Domestic and personal service	443	236
Barbers and hairdressers	59	3
Boarding and lodging house keepers	17	9
Inn and tavern keepers	128	22

Laborers, porters, helpers, etc.	239	200
Nurses and midwives	--	2
Trade and transportation	934	183
Bankers and brokers	27	1
Clerks and accountants	20	5
Draymen and carters	14	3
Hucksters and Peddlers	26	1
Merchants and dealers	779	57
Sea captains, mariners, mates, etc.	68	116
Manufacturing and mechanical pursuits	1,146	370
Bakers and confectioners	88	21
Blacksmiths	58	31
Brewers	15	2
Brickmakers and potters	11	1
Bricklayers	18	8
Butchers	30	5
Cabinetmakers	17	8
Carpenters and joiners		
House	166	43
Ship	3	76
Clock and watchmakers	12	1
Coopers	35	27
Goldsmiths and silversmiths	20	3
Harness and saddlemakers	30	1
Leather curriers and tanners	27	1
Mantuamakers and seamstresses	--	7
Metalworkers	34	1
Painters, glaziers, etc.	31	7
Plasterers	11	4
Printers, bookbinders, etc.	40	2
Ropemakers	5	16
Shoemakers	165	42
Stonecutters	8	4
Tailors	186	28
Textile workers	37	2
Tinmen	17	2
Weavers	2	17
Wheelwrights	13	2
Miscellaneous industries	67	7
Returned without occupation	676*	143**

*Includes 51 reported as "gentlemen."
**Includes 9 reported as gentlemen."

Source: W.S. Rossiter, *A Century of Population Growth; From the First Census of the United States to the Twelfth 1790-1900* (Washington, DC: U.S. Government Printing Office, 1909), pp. 142-143.

Three broad classes of occupations—agriculture, commerce, and manufactures—formed the basis for the first official occupational enumeration in the Census of 1820. These categories accord more with what we regard today as industrial classifications, but instructions to enumerators provided the basis for assigning specific occupations to each group. That census was enumerated on a family, rather than an individual, basis so that the census-takers indicated the number of each family who were principally engaged in each broad class of occupation (U.S. Bureau of the Census, 1904). Instructions to marshals explained:

> The discrimination between persons engaged in agriculture, commerce, and manufactures will not be without its difficulties. No inconsiderable portion of the population will probably be found, the individuals of which being asked to which of those classes they belong, will answer, to all three. Yet, it is obviously not the intention of the legislature that any one individual should be included in more than one of them — of those whose occupations are extensively agricultural or commercial, there can seldom arise a question, and in the column of manufactures will be included not only all the persons employed in what the act more specifically denominates manufacturing *establishments*, but all those artificers, handicraftsmen, and mechanics, whose labor is preeminently of the hand, and not upon the field."

There is no way to differentiate the specific occupations in 1820 since the enumerators recorded directly into the three broad categories. The usefulness of these general data was apparently questioned when plans for the Census of 1830 were developed and no occupational information was gathered at that time. By 1840, counts of occupational pursuits by families were resumed and the number of broad categories was extended to seven: Mining; agriculture; commerce; manufactures and trades; navigation of the ocean; navigation of canals, lakes and rivers; and learned professions and engineers. It was pointed out that the seven categories of employment in 1840 were more nearly representative of the whole body of workers than was the case in 1820, but servants and other persons rendering personal service were omitted, and government officials, clerks, and employees probably were not included.

A major change in the method of taking the Census of 1850 was a shift from family to individual enumeration. Also separate schedules were designed for free inhabitants and for slaves, a distinction not made in the previous censuses. The return of occupations in 1850 was limited to free males over 15 years of age, but occupational detail was increased considerably. It was now possible to distinguish 323 specific occupations, which were grouped under ten headings—commerce, trade, manufactures, mechanic arts, and mining; agriculture; labor, not agricultural; army; sea and river navigation; law, medicine, and divinity; other pursuits requiring education; government, civil service; domestic servants; other occupations (U.S. Bureau of the Census, 1904, xxxi).

By 1860, females as well as males, who were free inhabitants over 15 years of age, were asked their occupations. The increasing complexity of the employment sector and the diligence of census occupation specialists, resulted in identification of 584 detailed occupations.

In the Census of 1870, no age limit was specified on the schedule for reports of occupations, but enumerators were instructed to omit reports for infants or children too young to take any part in production. Effectively, the statistics reported were for persons 10 years of age and over, the age range observed in succeeding censuses. A reevaluation of occupational categories led to 338 being specified and these were classified under four headings—agriculture; professional and personal services; trade and transportation; and manufactures and mechanical and mining industries. In addition to returns for geographic areas, the published information was subdivided by sex, age and nationality.

During the succeeding decades, modifications in the coverage and classification of occupational data took place.

First, persons 10 years old and over were included in the inquiry through 1930, and the age limit was 14 years old and over in 1940 and later.

Second, beginning in 1910, separate reports on occupation and industry of workers were obtained. While the major categories remained industrial through 1930, occupations could be identified within them.

Third, the changing nature of work resulted in new nomenclature over the years and regrouping of occupational categories (Edwards, 1943; Conk, 1978). The emergence of new industries and occupations necessitated new titles and the gradual elimination of some old ones.

Fourth, the numbers of occupations which were detailed for presentation continued to change, being 265 in 1880, 218 in 1890, 303 in 1900, 428 in 1910, 572 in 1920, 534 in 1930, 451 in 1940, 469 in 1950, 494 in 1960, and 441 in 1970.

Fifth, a critical change in work concepts influenced the reporting of occupations in a significant way. Prior to 1870, it was not at all clear what the work status was of persons for whom occupations were reported. From 1870 to 1930, the view of work as the basis for deriving money income or the equivalent, and the traditional gender (sexual) division of labor occasioned the use of the concept "gainful work" as the foundation of occupational reporting. Persons who were "gainful workers" or "gainfully occupied" were those who usually earned money or a money equivalent, or who assisted in the production of marketable goods, whether or not they were employed at the time of the enumeration. Women who were "home-makers" working in their own homes without salaries or wages and having no other employment were excluded.

The inability to derive estimates of the currently unemployed from these data, a most unfortunate statistical limitation during the period of the severe economic depression of the 1930's, led to a revision of the basic work concepts. Some experimental surveys during the 1930's counted as unemployed those persons not working but "willing and able to work." Because of the subjectiveness of responses, it was difficult to compile data on the subject which were reliable and comparable over time and among places. As a result, the notion of a "labor force" and its components was developed for use in surveys and in the 1940 and later censuses: An individual's actual activity, that is, whether he or she was working, looking for work, or doing something else during the time reference of the inquiry became the principal criterion for classification (U.S. Bureau of the Census,, 1975.)

In general, the following major labor force components can be specified:

1. **Employed persons**—include (a) all those who, during the survey week, worked at all as paid employees, in their own business or profession or on their own farm, or who worked 15 hours or more as unpaid workers in an enterprise operated by a family member; and (b) all those who were not working but had jobs or businesses from which they were temporarily absent because of illness, bad weather, vacation, labor-management dispute, or personal reasons, whether or not they were paid by their employers for the time off, and whether or not they were seeking other jobs.

Each employed person is counted only once. Those who hold more than one job are counted in the job at which they worked the greatest number of hours during the survey week. Excluded are persons whose only activity consisted of work around the house or volunteer work for religious, charitable, and similar organizations.

2. **Unemployed persons**—comprise all persons who did not work during the survey week, who made specific efforts to find a job within the past 4 weeks, and who were available for work during the survey week except for temporary illness. Also included as unemployed are those who did not work at all, were available for work, and (a) were waiting to be called back to a job from which they had been laid off; (b) were waiting to report to a new wage or salary job within 30 days.

3. **The civilian labor force**—is the sum of employed and unemployed persons (14 years old and older through 1966, and persons 16 years old and older thereafter).

4. **The total labor force**—is the sum of the civilian labor force and the Armed Forces.

5. **Persons not in the labor force**—included all persons in the age range (14 years old and older, or in later years 16 years old and older) not classified as employed, unemployed, or in the Armed Forces.

With regard to occupational reporting under the labor force concept, distinctions can be made between current occupation of the employed, previous occupation of the unemployed, and last occupation (if ever employed) of those not in the labor force. In some surveys, information about multiple jobholders includes the different occupations in which they are engaged, and which one is the principal occupation.

The growing size and diversity of the labor force has made the description and classification of occupations exceedingly difficult. The detailed occupational list in the earlier censuses may have come close to describing the range of various jobs in the society at that time. Today we are presented with an extensive inventory of job-names, many of which most of us have never heard of or whose activities we would find difficult to describe. Some are colloquial terms, while others represent particular steps in a production, sales, or administrative process. So extensive is the list of job titles actually being used that the Bureau of the Census has designed a systematic procedure for translating described work activities into different levels of occupational classification. In preparation for the 1980 Census, two major indexes to occupations and industries were published, both as a guide to census clerks whose task is to code occupations and as a source of information for census data users (U.S. Bureau of the Census, 1980a, 1980b).

These indexes report about 29,000 occupational titles and 20,000 industry titles. They were grouped into 503 separate detailed occupational categories and then into 13 major groupings. In order to accomplish this, 3-digit numerical codes and some alphabetic codes were devised and each of the thousands of job titles were assigned to one of these. Some occupational titles are unique enough to suggest which code they fit into without any additional information (e.g., "Account auditor" is coded into "023 Accountants and Auditors"). However, some occupational titles require additional knowledge before their code can be determined. This is done by examining the industry classification and the class-of-worker category (i.e., employed by private organization, employed by public organization, self-employed, or working without pay in family business or farm). If these other criteria are helpful in making distinctions among occupations, the job title might be placed into one of the 503 categories which are described by a combination of occupation, industry, and class of worker (e.g., construction inspectors, public administration).

The Changing American Occupational Structure

At the same time that census categories of occupation were undergoing change because of an expanded economy, greater division of labor, and emergence of new work specialties, some noticeable shifts in the distribution of major occupational areas were taking place. In 1790 the nation was overwhelmingly agricultural; by now it has become predominantly industrialized and commercialized. During the interim, a profound transformation occurred which can be seen in the changing proportions in various occupational groupings.

Table 2-2. Per cent of Gainful Workers in Agriculture, 1820-1940

Year	Per cent in agriculture
1940	18.0
1920	27.0
1900	37.3
1880	50.1
1860	59.4
1840	82.2
1820	85.5

Source: U.S. Bureau of the Census, *Historical Statistics of the United States, Colonial Times to 1970,* Bicentennial Edition, Part 1 Washington, DC: U.S. Government Printing Office, 1975), p. 138.

The change from a largely rural to a largely urban population is reflected in the sharply declining percentage of gainful workers in agriculture (Table 2-2). From 86 per cent in 1820, the proportion fell below 60 per cent by 1860 and to 37 per cent by the turn of the century. The drop continued to 27 per cent in 1920 and to 18 per cent in 1940, when the "gainful worker" concept was last used officially in a census.

A review of trends in the occupational composition of the experienced civilian labor force since 1900 enables us to bring agricultural employment trends up to date as well as analyze overall occupational shifts during the period 1900-1980. As can be seen in Table 2-3, the percentage of male farmworkers, which had fallen from 42 per cent in 1900 to 22 per cent in 1940 (parallel to the decline in agricultural workers under the gainful employment concept), further dropped in succeeding decades until it had reached only 4 per cent in 1979.

Changes in the occupational structure for males were quite dramatic in the first eight decades of the twentieth century. In addition to the shift from farm to nonfarm work, some significant alterations in the composition of nonfarm work took place. Work in the service trades grew gradually from 3 to 9 per cent. The relative numbers of men in laboring jobs declined from 15 to 8 per cent, but operatives increased from 11 to 18 per cent, and craftsmen and related workers rose from 13 to 22 per cent. The most significant rise was observed for white-collar employment, which went from 18 per cent in 1900 to 41 per cent in 1979. Within this broader category, sales jobs increased modestly and clerical and managers, officials and proprietors rose somewhat more sharply. The most notable increase in white-collar work was for professional men, from 3 per cent of the male labor force in 1900 to 15 per cent in 1979. These trends for males indicate that the changing character of American society was well

Table 2-3. Per cent Distribution by Major Occupation Group of the Experienced Civilian Labor Force 14 and Over, by Sex: 1900 - 1979

Sex and major occupation group	1979	1970	1960	1950	YEAR: 1940	1930	1920	1910	1900
MALE: Total	100%	100%	100%	100%	100%	100%	100%	100%	100%
White collar workers	41	40	35	30	27	25	21	20	18
Professional, tech., & kindred workers	15	14	10	7	6	5	4	3	3
Managers, officials, and proprietors	14	11	11	10	9	9	8	8	7
Clerical and kindred workers	6	8	7	6	6	6	5	4	3
Salesworkers	6	7	7	6	6	6	5	5	5
Manual and service workers	57	56	56	55	52	50	48	45	41
Manual workers	48	48	50	48	46	45	44	41	38
Craftsmen, foremen, & kindred workers	22	21	21	19	15	16	16	14	13
Operative and kindred workers	18	20	21	21	18	15	14	13	11
Laborers, except farm and mine	8	7	8	9	12	14	14	15	15
Service workers	9	8	6	6	6	5	4	4	3
Private household workers	*	*	*	*	*	*	*	*	*
Service workers, exc. private household	9	8	6	6	6	5	4	4	3
Farmworkers	4	5	8	15	22	25	30	35	42
Farmers and farm managers	2	3	6	10	13	15	18	20	23
Farm laborers and foremen	2	2	3	5	8	10	12	15	19

*Less than 0.5 per cent.

Source: U.S. Bureau of the Census, *Historical Statistics of the United States, Colonial Times to 1970*, Bicentennial Edition, Part 1 (Washington, DC: U.S. Government Printing Office, 1975), pp. 139-140; U.S. Bureau of Labor Statistics, *Handbook of Labor Statistics*, Bulletin 2070 (Washington, DC: U.S. Government Printing Office, 1980).

Table 2-3. (Continued)

Sex and major occupation group	YEAR: 1979	1970	1960	1950	1940	1930	1920	1910	1900
FEMALE: Total	100%	100%	100%	100%	100%	100%	100%	100%	100%
White collar workers	64	61	56	52	45	44	39	26	18
Professional, tech., & kindred workers	16	15	13	12	13	14	12	10	8
Managers, officials, and proprietors	6	4	4	4	3	3	2	2	1
Clerical and kindred workers	35	35	31	27	21	21	19	9	4
Salesworkers	7	7	8	9	7	7	6	5	4
Manual and service workers	37	38	42	44	51	47	48	58	63
Manual workers	15	18	19	22	22	20	24	26	28
Craftsmen, foremen, & kindred workers	2	2	1	2	1	1	1	1	1
Operative and kindred workers	12	15	17	20	20	17	20	23	24
Laborers, except farm and mine	1	1	1	1	1	1	2	1	3
Service workers	21	20	23	21	29	27	24	32	35
Private household workers	3	4	8	9	18	18	16	24	29
Service workers, exc. private household	18	16	14	13	11	10	8	8	7
Farmworkers	1	1	2	4	4	8	14	16	19
Farmers and farm managers	*	*	1	1	1	2	3	4	6
Farm laborers and foremen	1	1	1	3	3	6	10	12	13

*Less than 0.5 per cent

Source: U.S. Bureau of the Census, *Historical Statistics of the United States, Colonial Times to 1970,* Bicentennial Edition, Part 1 (Washington, DC: U.S. Government Printing Office, 1975), pp. 139-140; U.S. Bureau of Labor Statistics, *Handbook of Labor Statistics,* Bulletin 2070 (Washington, DC: U.S. Government Printing Office, 1980).

reflected in a modification of the work force that accompanied an expanding technology and development of both government and private bureaucracies.

Although occupational trends have usually been examined for men only, it is clear that the increasing involvement of women in the labor force requires that attention be paid to their work trends as well. For one thing, the percentage of females in the labor force has risen sharply, from 18 per cent in 1890 to 52 per cent in 1980. Moreover, while women have been more likely to be engaged in part-time work, they have increasingly become full-time workers. Also with the passage of time, fewer and fewer occupations have remained the exclusive province of men.

Even during the period of time when men and women occupied essentially different labor force structures, the pattern and trends of occupational composition for the sexes were not too dissimilar. It has been the case that smaller proportions of employed females were found in farm work and that a much higher percentage were clerical workers (see Table 2-3), but it is probably also the case that many wives of farmers and farm laborers themselves were involved in farm work but regarded themselves as principally housewives and were so reported in the census.

Trends in the distribution of occupational groupings for women differed in some respects from that of men. For example, a notable drop in private household work was observed for females between 1900 and 1979 and sizable declines also took place in the operative category. On the other hand, similar trends by sex were apparent for farm work, other manual work, and white-collar occupations. By 1979, a comparison of men and women in the experienced civilian labor force showed a converging occupational composition but still showed significantly more women in clerical and service work and significantly more men in managerial and craft occupations.

William Hunt's Approach to Defining Status

To say that the American occupational structure has been undergoing profound change is not necessarily to say that socioeconomic status patterns have been changing in a like manner. Shifts in occupational composition may be indicative of newer technologies and forms of social organization which lead to improvements in output and emergence of new products which have little impact on the status of individuals. Moreover, when economies expand and become diversified, the society as a whole is affected. Hence, the status of workers and their dependents may remain unchanged.

When Madison, Jefferson, and others argued for the inclusion of data on occupations in the census, they apparently had in mind an inventory of types of work as well as a basis for estimating the social composition of the nation. With each successive census, the so-called occupational classification took on a decided industrial character, at least until the twentieth century. The major categories were types of industries which reflected the principal work complexes. Even when specific occupations were delineated in later censuses, they were grouped within the major industrial categories. Such captions as agriculture, mining, manufacturing, commerce, etc. identified the dominant industry-occupation combinations.

There is no evidence of any analysis of census data prior to the Census of 1870 which treated occupations in an explicit status framework, despite occasional references to the social characteristics of the population inherent in the industrial-occupational statistics.

William C. Hunt, a Department of Labor staff member, and later U.S. Bureau of the Census official, initiated a systematic analysis of occupational data for socioeconomic interpretation. In an issue of the Bulletin of the Department of Labor, Hunt (1897) reviewed the several tabluations of workers at gainful occupations in the Censuses of 1870, 1880, and 1890, and described the trends by age and sex, and for States over that period of time. He concluded

> that persons at work, especially females, have increased very much faster than the population at large; that as a result the proportion of workers relative to the total population and to the whole number of persons of the respective ages was considerably greater in 1890 than at the preceding census periods, and that this increased proportion is apparent for each of the great classes of occupations, with the single exception of agriculture, fisheries, and mining.

Hunt realized that the existing occupational groupings did not "afford an altogether satisfactory basis" for comparing the status of occupations, and he decided to regroup the specific occupations "into four great groups designated as A, B, C, and D." Each of the great groupings had subcategories (4 in group A, 2 in group B, 12 in group C, and 9 in group D). The essential criterion for grouping and subgrouping was Hunt's understanding of "the character of the employment." According to the author

> "Group A relates to what may be termed the proprietor class, comprising farmers, planters, bankers, brokers, manufacturers, merchants and dealers, professional people, and those of kindred pursuits; Group B relates to what may be termed the clerical class, comprising agents, collectors, commercial travelers, bookkeepers, clerks, salesmen, and other clerical occupations; Group C to what may be termed skilled workers, comprising, so far as the census figures admit of such distinctions, those occupations or groups of occupations in which skilled labor plays the principal part, such as clothing makers, engineers and firemen (not locomotive), food preparers, leather workers, those engaged in the mechanical trades, metal workers, printers, engravers, book-binders, steam-railroad employees, textile workers, tobacco and cigar factory operatives, wood workers, and similar mechanical pur-

suits; and Group D relates to what may be termed, for want of a better designation, the laboring class, comprising those employments which are, as a rule, the more laborious, and in which the bulk of the work done does not call for a high degree of mechanical skill or ability, such as agricultural laborers, boatmen, fishermen, pilots, sailors, draymen, hostlers, street-railway employees, laborers (not specified, miscellaneous manufacturing pursuits, messengers, packers, porters, miners, quarrymen, servants, and the like."

Following detailed analysis of trends from 1870 to 1890 in these various groupings and sub-groupings, separately for men, women, and children, Hunt arrived at the general finding that "in spite of this growing disinclination toward agriculture and notwithstanding that our great manufacturing and commercial centers have become very much crowded in recent years,...the increased proportion of workers is found generally in the higher walks of business life and in those occupations which call for skilled labor principally rather than in the lowest or more laborious forms of employment." He concluded, therefore, "that the great body of workers has, as a whole, progressed and has perceptibly risen in the social scale of life."

This innovative effort to translate census statistics into a summary of the social condition of the country set a precedent for later attempts to attach socioeconomic meaning to occupational data. It also provided an acknowledgment that occupations might be used as indexes for varying styles of life in addition to representing kinds of work activity. This distinction between work activity and socioeconomic status has continued to plague census and other government officials who collect, classify, and present occupational statistics, because occupations are still regarded mainly as components of a labor force structure which aid in the interpretation of trends in employment and unemployment while also being indicators of the nation's social stratification (Scoville, 1972). As Hunt demonstrated, different groupings of specific occupations will serve each purpose better.

The scheme for grouping occupations into four broad social strata, as devised by Hunt, was incorporated by census historian Carroll D. Wright (1899) in his turn-of-the century textbook on sociology, but there is no indication that it was adopted by others. It remained for later governmental employees and students of social stratification to revise and update Hunt's procedures as a means of portraying the country's social condition and the disparity of statuses among individuals and families.

Alba Edwards' Scheme of Occupational Classification

Despite the fact that censuses had been conducted in the U.S. since 1790, the U.S. Bureau of the Census as a governmental agency was not created until 1902. Before then, the census function was incorporated in other departments of the federal government. The new agency built up its staff very slowly, and most of its employees had very general responsibilities. In 1909, in preparation for the upcoming decennial census, additional staff were added. Among them was Alba M. Edwards, whose principal responsibility was in the area of occupations and other data on workers. Edwards became familiar with Hunt's work on occupational groupings and saw ways of improving on the scheme. In particular he felt that recognition of social strata should be included in census reports directly and not just be relegated to other governmental and professional publications.

Edwards proceeded with his clasificatory efforts for several years, after which he published his seminal article on "Social-Economic Groups of the United States" in the *Journal of American Statistical Association*. In discussing the bases for his groupings, Edwards (1917) pointed out that

> There are those who desire a grouping of occupations according to skill. In many respects such a grouping, if it could be carried out, would be an admirable and a useful one; but a complete grouping of occupations according to skill is impossible, since many occupations do not lend themselves to such a grouping. For example, proprietors usually are distinguished from the other workers in the same industry or business, not by a difference in skill but rather by a difference in the possession of property, credit, and business and executive ability ... In fact, in a grouping such as here presented, we can properly classify according to skill only those occupations in which the expenditure of muscular force is one of the chief characteristics. It is impossible, of course, to draw a hard and fast line between those occupations which are characterized chiefly by the exercise of muscular force or manual dexterity, and those which are characterized chiefly by the exercise of mental force of ingenuity. In other words, it is impossible to draw a hard and fast line between the hand workers and the head workers. But such a line may be drawn sufficiently accurately for our purpose.

The roughly 428 occupations specified in the census of 1910 were then grouped into nine categories, as follows:

I. Proprietors, officials, and managers
II. Clerks and kindred workers
III. Skilled workers
IV. Semi-skilled workers
V. Laborers
VI. Servants
VII. Public officials
VIII. Semi-official public employees
IX. Professional persons

Since there was no empirical basis for determining the assignment of specific occupations to each of the categories (other socioeconomic information not yet being included in the census returns), the groupings were based solely on Edwards' opinion as to where they should be placed. He separated workers whose jobs were chiefly characterized by muscular force using the following criteria:

> those occupations have been considered skilled for the pursuance of which a long period of training or an apprenticeship usually is necessary, and which in their pursuance call for a degree of judgment and manual dexterity, one or both, above that required in semiskilled occupations. Those occupations have been considered semiskilled for the pursuance of which only a short period or no period of preliminary training is necessary, and which in their pursuance call for only a moderate degree of judgment or of manual dexterity. Laborers have been considered to include those occupations the workers in which require no special training, judgment, or manual dexterity, but supply mainly muscular strength for the performance of coarse, heavy work.

Edwards used his classification to describe occupational status trends from 1870 to 1910, extending the approach of Hunt for two more decades and elaborating the classification scheme. For sixteen more years, this renowned statistician continued to study the nature of occupations and the similarities and differences among jobs. In 1933, he again published an article in the *Journal of the American Statistical Association* in which he presented his revised groupings of gainful workers:

1. Professional persons
2. Proprietors, managers, and officials
   2-a. Farmers (owners and tenants)
   2-b. Wholesale and retail dealers
   2-c. Other proprietors, managers, and officals
3. Clerks and kindred workers
4. Skilled workers and foremen
5. Semi-skilled workers
   5-a. Semi-skilled workers in manufacturing
   5-b. Other semi-skilled workers
6. Unskilled workers
   6-a. Farm laborers
   6-b. Factory and building construction laborers
   6-c. Other laborers
   6-d. Servant classes

It is clear from the groupings that Edwards was influenced not only by added knowledge and insights which he acquired in studying occupations but also by changes in the nature of work and in ocupational shifts which had been occurring in the society. Contemporary students of occupational classification will recognize this 1933 scheme as a forerunner of the contemporary U.S. census grouping of occupations in official reports. At the same time, these classifications are now referred to as "major occupational groups" with no suggestion that they represent social-economic groupings.

Up until 1938, the Bureau of the Census refrained from including

Edward's social-economic groupings in a government publication. In that year, an official Census publication was issued which summarized the scheme first presented in 1933 and reported historical statistics on the subject (Edwards, 1938). The approach and the data seemed to be especially suitable for President Roosevelt's New Deal social programs, and Edward's work of many years was given official sanction. In this monograph, Edwards called attention to his belief that the groupings not only comprised distinct social-economic strata but also "are arranged approximately in descending order of the social-economic status of the workers comprising them." It is this aspect of the scheme that has been most controversial in the social stratification literature.

The 1940 Census was the first to use the "labor force" concept and comparability with earlier "gainful worker" data was impaired. In order to restore comparability with earlier data, a major publication of the 1940 Census series, designed and written by Alba Edwards, was prepared. It included three parts: Comparison of occupation and industry statistics for 1930 and 1940 with adjustment of "gainful worker" data to the "labor force" basis; comparable occupation statistics for the period 1870 to 1930; and a social economic grouping of the nation's labor force from 1910 to 1940. The first two parts provided data of greatest interest to analysts of the work force, and the last part was of most significance to those concerned with social status trends and patterns.

In the preface to this publication, Edwards (1943) offered the statement which has become one of the most often cited references in the social science literature. He wrote:

> The most nearly dominant single influence in a man's life is probably his occupation. More than anything else, perhaps, a man's occupation determines his course and his contribution in life. And when life's span is ended, quite likely there is no other single set of facts that will tell so well the kind of man he was and the part he played in life as will a detailed and chronological statement of the occupation, or occupations, he pursued. Indeed, there is no other single characteristic that tells so much about a man and his status — social, intellectual, and economic — as does his occupation. A man's occupation not only tells, for each workday, what he does during one-half of his waking hours, but it indicates, with some degree of accuracy, his manner of life during the other half — the kind of associates he will have, the kind of clothes he will wear, the kind of house he will live in, and even, to some extent, the kind of food he will eat. And, usually, it indicates, in some degree, the cultural level of his family.

The definitions and statistics of socio-economic groupings included in the 1940 Census volume constituted the first presentation of that material in a report of the census. Concepts used by Edwards in this 1938 monograph were carried forward into the 1940 Census report. Each of the six hierarchically arranged major groupings was described in terms of the similarity of characteristics of specific occupations within a group and the difference in characteristics of specific occupations between groups. The relative homogeneity of the groups, from a socio-economic point of view, was thus tentatively established.

In response to existing and anticipated criticisms of the groupings as constituting a graduated scale of socioeconomic measurement, Edwards (1943, 80) argued that

> The workers in each group have been included partly because of their social and partly because of their economic status. The standard — if it be a standard — is thus a hybrid — partly social and partly economic. And the weight of the social factor varies from one group to another, and from one occupation to another, as does, also, the weight of the economic factor. Thus, the social factor is of greater weight in the clerical group than in the skilled group, but the reverse is true as to the economic factor.

He went on to support his reasoning by showing data on education ("a very large factor in the social status of workers") and money income ("a very large factor in their economic status"), the distribution of each tabulated by the six social-economic groupings of occupations. Relying primarily on median years of school completed and median wage or salary income, he indicated that the social-economic groups are arranged in "descending order of the social-economic status of the workers comprising them and that they do constitute a scale," while admitting that there was a wide range among occupations within each group in education and income.

Edwards (1943, 182) was somewhat prophetic of later extensions of his work when he stated:

> With increased accuracy in the original census data, and with more nearly exact classification of these data by occupation, education, and income, it will be possible to refine the context of the respective groups and thus to make them a more nearly exact and satisfactory scale for the measurement of census and other occupation data.

The Alba Edwards social-economic groupings of occupations, and approximations of them, have been liberally used and cited in social science research. It has only been in recent years, when more refined approaches have indeed been used, that the Edwards' classification has given way to newer occupational scales and indexes. However, the scheme has served two general purposes in social research. On the one hand, it has permitted analysts to sketch the outline of the social structure through a description of the distribution of social classes at a given point in time, and changes in the distribution from period to period. On the other hand, the designation of specific occupations as falling within broader social strata made it possible for reseachers to gather occupational information for respondents in surveys, or from various records, and assign individuals with reported occupations to the designated strata. It is probably this latter usage which has made the status groupings of occupations so popular as a technique of research in recent years.

Other Status Variables in Census Enumeration

Substantial reliance on occupational data to measure status does not mean that other status indicators were absent from the census. Various educational, economic, and housing variables have been included in census questionnaires, particularly in more recent decades (U.S. Bureau of the Census, 1971, 1975). These variables have been used as direct indicators of status, they have been employed to provide an index of the status of occupations, and they have been combined to form multiple-item indicators of status.

Data on literacy, the ability to read and write in some language, was first collected in 1840 and was obtained in each census through 1930. The distinction between literate and illiterate persons, while not a significant one in recent years, did differentiate substantial proportions of the population in earlier decades.

School enrollment statistics have been included in each census since 1850. Although applying mainly to younger persons, school-going has been a characteristic generally associated with social status and is the basis for educational attainment.

The principal measure of educational attainment-years of school completed-was first part of the Census of 1940 and has been collected ever since. It can be relevant for every adult who has passed school and college ages, and thus is a meaningful achievement measure for the whole population.

The Census of 1940 was also the first one in which wage and salary data were obtained for individuals, and it provided the debut for an item on the value of rented, owned, and vacant housing units. The money value of jobs and residences thereby became a potential ingredient in status calculations. Both sets of statistics have been continued to the present, but since 1940 the total income of individuals and families has been reported which incorporates specific types of income other than wages and salaries.

The 1950 Census extended status-related measurement of housing variables by including an interviewer-determined rating of house condition as well as the condition of selected housing facilities and various indicators of home equipment. Many of these have been combined by researchers into a housing scale or index which is related to other status variables.

The availability of these several measures of social status, especially in recent years, has made it possible to construct alternatives to occupation alone as an indicator of status from census data in addition to laying the basis for more refined status placement of occupations.

REFERENCES

Conk, Margo A. 1978. "Occupational Classification in the United States: 1870-1940." *Journal of Interdisciplinary History* 9: 111-130.

Edwards, Alba M. 1917. "Social-Economic Groups of the United States." *Quarterly Journal of the American Statistical Association* 15: 643-644.

Edwards, Alba M. 1933. "A Social-Economic Grouping of the Gainful Workers of the United States." *Journal of the American Statistical Association* 28: 378.

Edwards, Alba M. 1938. *A Social-Economic Grouping of the Gainful Workers of the United States.* Washington, DC: U.S. Government Printing Office.

Edwards, Alba M. 1943. *Comparative Occupation Statistics for the United States, 1870 to 1940,* sixteenth Census of the United States, 1940, Population. Washington, DC: U.S. Government Printing Office.

Gales, Joseph, Sr. 1834. *Annals of Congress; Debates and Proceedings in the Congress of the United States, vol. 1.* Washington, DC: Gales and Seaton, pp. 1077-1078.

Hamilton, Alexander, *et al.* 1937. *The Federalist; A Commentary on the Constitution of the United States,* no. 56. New York: Modern Library.

Hunt, William C. 1897. "Workers at Gainful Occupations at the Federal Censuses of 1870, 1880, and 1890." *Bulletin of the Department of Labor,* no. 11: 415.

Padover, Saul K. 1943. *The Complete Jefferson.* New York: Duell, Sloan & Pearce, pp. 998-999.

Rossiter, W.S. 1909. *A Century of Population Growth; From the First Census of the United States to the Twelfth 1790-1900.* Washington, DC: U.S. Government Printing Office, p. 42.

Scoville, James G. 1972. *Manpower and Occupational Analysis: Concepts and Measurements,* Part 1. Lexington, MA: D.C. Heath.

U.S. Bureau of the Census. 1904. *Twelfth Census of the United States, 1900, Special Reports, Occupations.* Washington, DC: U.S. Government Printing Office, p. xxix.

U.S. Bureau of the Census. 1971. *Census of Housing, 1970, General Housing Characteristics, United States Summary.* Washington, DC: U.S. Government Printing Office, App. 7 to App. 9.

U.S. Bureau of the Census. 1975. *Historical Statistics of the United States, Colonial Times to 1970, Bicentennial Edition.* Washington, DC: U.S. Government Printing Office, chapters F, H, and N.

U.S. Bureau of the Census. 1980a. *1980 Census of Population: Alphabetical Index of Industries and Occupations.* Washington, DC: U.S. Government Printing Office.

U.S. Bureau of the Census. 1980b. *1980 Census of Population: Classified Index of Industries and Occupations.* Washington, DC: U.S. Government Printing Office.

Wright, Carroll D. 1899. *Outline of Practical Sociology.* New York: Longmans, Green, pp. 254-255.

Wright, Carroll D. 1900. *The History and Growth of the United States Census.* Washington, DC: U.S. Government Printing Office, p. 20.

3
Occupation as a Sole Socioeconomic Status Indicator

While the history of the United States Census shows that a variety of social status indicators have been included among the many decennial inquiries, it also reveals that occupation has been the status indicator most frequently included in the census. Moreover, census occupational data have most often been used as a sole indicator to mark an individual's place in the social hierarchy.

The work of Alba Edwards (1943) in developing a set of occupational categories which purported to form a social scale, and the incorporation of such work in the census tabulations and publications emanating from subsequent censuses, provided the basis for the use of occupation as a sole status indicator. Even those researchers who have criticized the assumptions on which the Edwards scale was formed, and who sometimes have altered the methodology for scaling used by Edwards, have agreed that one's occupation is a better index of status than any other variable that can be obtained from a census enumeration.

It was long recognized, both within and outside the Census Bureau, that the major occupational classification (about eleven broad categories) derived from Edward's work and being used in the census constituted at best a very crude status scale. A number of decades passed, however, before any serious attempt was made to review the existing scheme of occupations for purposes of status analysis and to propose an alternative basis for estimating the status of persons in given occupations.

In the late 1950's, as preliminary work for the 1960 Census was being carried out, it was agreed that the occupational classifications as presented in census tabluations and reports did not constitute the best basis for comprehending the social stratification of the nation and yet, in the absence of more useful schemes, data users would probably continue to employ the occupational statistics that were made available as a means for describing social strata.

The growing literature on social stratification, noted in Chapter 1, reflected advances in theory and methodology about social status. Census staff agreed to apply this new knowledge to improve the measurement of status. Moreover, the addition of time-tested census questions on education and income to those on occupation meant that it was no longer necessary to rely solely on judgments or opinion about occupations in order to estimate their status value. A range of possibilities for the construction of new measures existed. There was clearly a need for status-based measures which could mirror the objective social conditions of various segments of the society and enable academic researchers and government groups to indicate socioeconomic disparitites in the country and their variations and trends. It was agreed that it was incumbent upon the Bureau of the Census to provide data users with the most meaningful social information possible.

Charles Nam, Paul Glick, Edward Stockwell, and later Mary Powers, among the Bureau's professional staff, were involved in frequent discussions and exchanges of memoranda about these matters. It was decided that a new occupational status scheme linked to the census should be developed.

It took some time for acceptance of the effort to permeate all levels of the Bureau. At first, experimentation was encouraged with no guarantee that the results would ever be officially supported, much less published by the agency. As news of the corresponding occupational research by Otis Dudley Duncan (1961) became known, however, the interest of the Bureau increased. Duncan's aim was to develop a set of scores that could be used to assign status levels to detailed census occupational categories, the same thing the Bureau staff was trying to do. However, Duncan was basing his approach partly on information external to the census whereas Nam and associates were planning to rely wholly on census information for input to measurement. Futhermore, Duncan was using a study of prestige evaluations of occupations as a criterion for establishing his scores, whereas the Bureau's staff insisted on a more objective, socioeconomic basis for their calculations. As a result of frank exchanges and subsequent Bureaus considerations, authorization was given to proceed with plans for a new occupational status measure.

In fact, the Bureau's plan was more comprehensive than a new measure of occupational status alone. It called for a multiple-item measure of socioeconomic status. (This more extensive approach will be discussed in Chapter 4.) But one element of the new socioeconomic measurement was an occupational status indicator, and it is this feature which we will discuss in the remainder of this chapter.

The development of these occupational status scores from census data requires a series of steps, each of which can have a profound impact on the resulting scores themselves. There are issues concerning the reporting and coding of occupations, how specific occupations are grouped, what criteria are used to rate occupations, and procedures for calculating the scores. Discussion of each of these steps now follows.

Reporting and Coding of Occupations

In simple societies whose social structures are relatively undifferentiated, the number and variety of work roles are small and the occupations which can be described are relatively few. In a society as complex as that of the United States, the workforce is large and the division of labor quite elaborate. To describe the occupations included in the U.S. labor force is, therefore, an imposing task.

The fourth edition of the ***Dictionary of Occupational Titles***(DOT) (U.S. Department of Labor, 1977) includes descriptions of job duties for about 20,000 occupations. Compared with the third edition (U.S. Department of Labor, 1965), more than 2,100 new occupational definitions were added and over 3,500 were deleted, reflecting the dynamic aspect of the labor force. Each occupation is given a unique 9-digit code and is described in terms of training time, aptitudes, interests, temperaments, physical demands, working conditions, work performed, and industry.

The data for this expansive effort were derived from some 75,000 on-site job analyses of the spectrum of jobs in various industries, as determined by specialists in a number of State Employment Service Occupational Analysis Field Centers affiliated with the U.S. Employment Service. The numerous occupational titles were grouped into categories identified by 3-digit codes based on types of occupations.

A National Research Council committee assigned to evaluate the DOT concluded that there was a strong and continuing need for this kind of information but that substantial improvements in the procedures and products of the program were required for occupational information purposes (Miller et al., 1980).

A related attempt to organize the vast number of work roles into a more limited array of occupational categories has been the Standard Occupational Classification (SOC) (U.S. Department of Commerce, 1980). Because various governmental agencies used different occupational classification systems, there was a need to standardize occupation-related data collected by social and economic statistical reporting programs. The Classification provides a 4-digit coding system and nomenclature for identifying and classifying occupations with a framework suitable for use in and out of government. All of the items listed in the Dictionary of Occupational Titles can be encompassed within the categories of the Standard Occupational Classification.

When a census is taken, it is required that information on occupation be recorded, coded, and classified in some systematic manner. The Dictionary of Occupational Titles and Standard Occupational Classification provide criteria for translating the myriad types of work reported into occupational data for census use. However, the traditional uses of census data make it necessary for a somewhat modified version of occupational coding and classification. It has been the practice for the Bureau to code occupations on the basis of responses to several census inquiries related to work status. The block of questions for this purpose used in the 1980 Census is reproduced in Figure 3-1 on Page 46.

Information is solicited about the company and type of business or industry in which the individual worked, the kind of work and job duties as well as occupational title, and the classification of worker (public, private, or self-employment). This range of data is used in combination to arrive at an appropriate occupational designation.

Expert coders are employed to digest the information and assign a 3-digit number or letter industry code and a 3-digit number or letter occupational code to the individual, using indexes of industries and occupations specially devised for the census operation (U.S. Bureau of the Census, 1980a, 1980b). The indexes incorporate 19,000 industry and 23,000 occupational titles discovered historically in a review of census and survey schedules and supplemented by reference to the Dictionary of Occupational Titles. That the Census Index includes more occupational titles than the Dictionary list indicates that some jobs have alternative titles, frequently in colloquial terms, which are entered on the census or survey forms.

Occupational Groupings

For most purposes, whether it be research or job placement or other occupation-related activities, maintenance of 20,000 or more occupational distinctions would not be very useful. As already indicated, one element of each occupational reporting system has been the classification of the many occupations into smaller sets. Reductions in the number of categories have varied among the different systems.

The 9-digit codes of the Dictionary of Occupational Titles enables one to sort occupations in several ways. The first three digits identify a particular occupational group. All occupations are clustered into one of nine broad categories (first digit), such as professional, technical and managerial, or clerical and sales occupations. These categories break down into 82 occupationally-specific divisions (first two digits), such as occupations in architecture and engineering within the professional category, or stenography, typing, filing and related occupations in the clerical and sales category. Divisions, in turn, separate into small, homogeneous groups (first three digits), 559 such groups being identified in the DOT classification. The middle three digits of the 9-digit code describes the relationship of the worker to data, people, and things, respectively. The last three digits indicate the alphabetical

Figure 3-1: Block of Questions Related to Work Status Used in 1980 U.S. Census

33–35. Current or most recent job activity

Describe clearly this person's chief job activity or business last week, if any. If he had more than one job, describe the one at which he worked the most hours.

If this person had no job or business last week, give information for last job or business since 1960.

33. Industry

a. For whom did he work? *If now on active duty in the Armed Forces, print "AF" and skip to question 36.*

(Name of company, business, organization, or other employer)

b. What kind of business or industry was this?
Describe activity at location where employed.

(For example: Junior high school, retail supermarket, dairy farm, TV and radio service, auto assembly plant, road construction)

c. Is this mainly— *(Fill one circle)*

- ○ Manufacturing
- ○ Wholesale trade
- ○ Retail trade
- ○ Other *(agriculture, construction, service, government, etc.)*

34. Occupation

a. What kind of work was he doing?

(For example: TV repairman, sewing machine operator, spray painter, civil engineer, farm operator, farm band, junior high English teacher)

b. What were his most important activities or duties?

(For example: Types, keeps account books, files, sells cars, operates printing press, cleans buildings, finishes concrete)

c. What was his job title?

35. Was this person— *(Fill one circle)*

Employee of private company, business, or individual, for wages, salary, or commissions . . . ○

Federal government employee . . . ○
State government employee . . . ○
Local government employee *(city, county, etc.)* . . . ○

Self-employed in own business, professional practice, or farm—
Own business not incorporated . . . ○
Own business incorporated . . . ○

Working without pay in family business or farm ○

order of titles within the 6-digit code groups.

The Standard Occupational Classification list is structured on a four-level system: Division, major group, minor group, and unit group. Each level represents groupings in successively finer detail which enables users to tabulate or analyze data on different levels of aggregation. Thus, the division of "service occupations" includes the major group of "protective serivce occupations," which includes the minor group of "police and detectives" which in turn includes the unit group of "correctional institution officers."

An optimum occupational classification system is one in which a parsimonious set of categories is presented without severely reducing the homogeneity of individual categories. By using several levels of categorization, the level of homogeneity acceptable for particular analyses can be chosen. In the 1970 Census, the thousands of specific occupations were combined into 441 separate categories which can be reduced to 12 major groups. For some census tabulations and publications, an intermediate occupational list was also devised which covers 158 categories for males and 86 categories for females. A more condensed list contained 32 categories for total employed and 22 categories for employed females.

The ultimate objective in the status scoring procedure for occupations that we devised was to assign ratings for specific occupations that were essentially homogeneous with regard to occupational characteristics. One difficulty with the major groupings is that they are extremely heterogeneous with regard to types of specific occupations. The detailed occupational list for the census includes a manageable number of occupations which retain a fair degree of homogeneity. Since even each detailed occupation subsumes occupations of greater specificity, or masks variations in work status according to seniority, responsibility, skill level, and other characteristics, some heterogeneity remains. (In the following chapter, we will discuss one approach to further reducing that heterogeneity for purposes of status analysis.) However, we relied on the detailed occupational categories of the census as the occupational groups for which we wished to develop status indicators. (The detailed occupational lists are presented in the Appendices along with the scores calculated for them for the 1970 census period.)

Criteria for Rating Occupations

A major finding of the socioeconomic leterature review in Chapter 1 was that there are important distinctions between occupational status and occupational prestige, and quite often the two concepts are mistakenly regarded as synonomous (Treas and Tyree, 1979). Occupational status refers to the objective socioeconomic conditions associated with holding a particular occupation, whereas occupational prestige refers to the subjective evaluations people have of the social standing of an occupation. The prestige of an occupation depends, in part, on its status level, although other factors may also weigh heavily. The status of an occupation may change in time as a partial consequene of its prestige, even though other variables may be its principal determinants.

Studies have shown that the subjective *prestige* dimension of occupations is assigned by the public on the basis of a number of occupational attributes—the degree of interesting and challenging work, intelligence required, scarcity of qualified personnel, the originality and initiative associated with the work, level of influence over others, training and education required, job security, income received, how honorable and moral the work is, what it contributes to humanity, and other traits (Garbin and Bates, 1961). In terms of broader classifications of these traits, intellectual and training requirements as well as rewards of the work are extremely important, but also of substantial significance are characteristics such as interpersonal relations provided and the intrinsic nature of the work.

When one considers the elements of occupational *status*, on the other hand, it appears that the relevant factors are related to the general life style associated with holding the occupations. These are traditionally regarded as being composed of the objective imputs to attainment of the occupation and the objective outputs accruing to the occupational incumbents. While family background, political influence, other group memberships, and various forms of discrimination may enter into the determinations, the two elements usually identified as essential determinants of occupationsl status are education and income (Pavalko, 1971; Reiss, 1961). Research has also shown that residential location and housing status are related to occupational status, but these may be viewed as indirect effects of income level attained.

We were thus guided by the earlier work of others in relying upon measures of education and income to gauge occupational status. It remained for us to determine which measures of each variable to use. Our decision was to select the median level of years of school completed and the median level of total individual income for the aggregate of persons in each detailed occupation. In doing this, we were rejecting as inadequate for our purpose other possible items such as components of income. In fact, the original census tabulations we had to rely on provided a distribution of years of schooling for each occupational category and a distribution of total individual income. Had there been tabulations by earnings, we might have used them instead of total income, although there are persuasive arguments for treating non-earnings income as a real outcome of one's occupational status.

The calculation of a median measure for each variable instead of an arithmetic mean or other average tendency was based on the distributions of the variables, particularly income, which are skewed. As a consequence of the distributional property, the mean would portray an average which was unrealistically high. The median, on the other hand, would divide the occupational aggregate in half. The median was also deemed preferable to a specific distributional statistic. The Duncan SEI, for example, is based on the per cent in an occupation who had completed 4 years of high school or beyond and the per cent with $3,500 or more of individual income in a year. With the passage of time, these indicators will move further away from the statistical average. When our occupational scores are recalculated at a later point in time, continued use of the median indicates that the occupation is characterized by the average educational and income levels as of that period. In Duncan's scheme, new indicators need to be developed and standardization over time may thereby be compromised.

The fact that only a single indicator of each item is used ignores the variability in levels of education and income for persons in each occupation. Both the Duncan SEI and ours can therefore be regarded as characterizing the typical status of occupations and not necessarily of the individuals who occupy them. (In the next chapter, we shall deal with this problem as we describe our multiple-item index for individuals.)

Correlates of Occupational Status and Their Relation to the Scores

The occupational status level in our scheme is determined primarily by the relative education and income levels of the detailed occupations. That is, assignment of a score for the occupation depends on the relative position of the median for that occupation in the array of medians for all occupations. As we shall see when the actual procedure for scoring is elaborated, a third ingredient for determining the status score is the number of persons in the occupation.

Other factors which might have been incorporated as input to the score itself include measures of the age composition, racial composition, sex ratio, and residence of the occupational incumbents. The input might have taken the form of controls introduced through demographic standardization techniques. Age was used as a control for standardization of the Duncan SEI, for example. After careful consideration, we decided not to build these items into the score itself. Obviously, occupational status does vary among these subcategories of the population. We were attempting to develop nationwide standards of occupational status, however, and to the extent that occupational status varied across subcategories, these were patterns we wished to observe when we analyzed the resulting data. If we had incorporated the subcategories into the index itself, we could not have observed the variations. Also, it would always be possible for analysts who wished to do so to control for these correlates statistically in the process of performing their analyses.

Procedures for Calculating the Scores

The occupational status scores were first calculated for males 14 years of age and older in the experienced civilian labor force in 1950, largely because the required education and income data for each detailed occupation were already tabulated and published for that category of the population. Comparable data for females or for other labor force groups were not available then.

The actual procedure involved:

a) arraying detailed occupations (which in some cases, are occupation-industry-class of worker combinations) according to the median *educational* level of the incumbents.

b) arraying the same occupations separately according to the median *income* level of the incumbents,

c) by using the number of persons engaged in each occupation, determining the cumulative interval of persons in each occupation for each of the two arrays, beginning with the lowest-ranked occupation, and

d) averaging the midpoints of the two cumulative intervals of occupants and dividing by the total male experienced civilian labor force to get a status score for the occupation.

For example, if there were 50 million males in the experienced civilian labor force, of whom one million were in occupation Y, and the median educational level was higher for occupations containing 35 million persons and lower for occupations containing 14 million persons, the cumulative interval of persons for occupation Y in the education array would be 14,000,001—15,000,000.

If, in the above example, the cumulative interval for the income array were 17,000,001—18,000,000, then 14,500,000, the midpoint on the education scale, plus 17,500,000, the midpoint on the income scale, would average to 16,000,000, be divided by 50,000,000, the total number in the male experienced civilian labor force, and result in a score for occupation Y of 32.

The occupational status scores thus derived can take values between 0 and 100, and a score indicates the approximate percentage of males in the experienced civilian labor force who are in occupations having combined average levels of education and income below that for the given occupation. Therefore, this procedure leads to a simple and understandable interpretation of the status score not found with regard to other status measures. Also, while the score is the property of an occupation (being an average tendency for persons in that occupation), the number of occupational incumbents has some influence on the exact score and its use as a weight permits the interpretation of the scores as indicated. This feature of the scores commends it as well for time trend analysis, as will be shown subsequently.

A comment should be made on our failure to introduce any weighting of the education and income components before reckoning an occupational score. Since ours was not a prestige-based measure, and we had no independent criterion of status, we simply averaged the values for the two components. Other studies lend support for that decision (Coleman and Rainwater, 1978), although the matter should be reviewed and the advantages of introducing weights matched with the disadvantages of compromising historical comparability of the scores.

Alternative Sets of Scores

The set of occupational status scores first developed using this procedure (U.S. Bureau of the Census, 1963) will not serve all research purposes well because it is based on data as of 1950 and relates only to males in the labor force. Fortunately, the methodology which was employed permitted Nam and Powers to replicate the scores fairly easily for later years and other population groups. Most of these alternative sets of scores have been published elsewhere (Nam and Powers, 1968; Nam, LaRocque, Powers and Holmberg, 1975; Powers and Holmberg, 1978). The set based on 1970, and differentiated for males, females, females who are full-time year-round workers, and both sexes combined, are presented in Appendix Table A1. It is anticipated that 1980-based scores for various groups will be calculated when the requisite census data become available (probably in the mid-1980's).

Each set of scores is based upon data unique for that population and time. Hence, even though the same procedures were used to derive the scores in each case, the scores from different sets cannot be mixed. That is, a researcher wanting to make use of the scores to classify occupations socioeconomically should select the set of scores which best fits the population and time-period being analyzed. If, for example, the group for whom occupational reports are being analyzed are wholly or predominantly males and the data relate to near the year 1970, then that set of scores might be selected. If, on the other hand, occupational information is given for both males and females and the data are for a year near 1970, the set of scores for both sexes should be chosen. It can be noted that the scores for most occupations do not vary greatly, especially if the 2-digit scores are collapsed into fewer categories for analysis. Later chapters of this volume discuss differences in occupational status over time and among population subcategories.

Examination of the occupational detail for different census years will show that it varies between 1970 and the earlier years. In fact, the Bureau of the Census revises its detailed occupational list for each census. Some occupations formerly shown separately are combined, some occupations are divided into two or more categories, and new occupations are recognized that had not been designated earlier. About nine-tenths of the detailed occupational titles were the same in 1950 and 1960. The detail presented for 1950 and 1960 in our earlier reports are the same, however, because at the time the 1960 scores were developed, the two occupational lists were calibrated to facilitate comparative analysis. The occupational detail for 1970 was considerably different from that of the earlier years (only one-fourth of the titles capable of being matched), so we retained the reported detail for 1970.

Note should also be taken of the absence of certain expected categories on the list. Because the population covered refers to the experienced civilian labor force (involving activities tied to the production of goods and services for pay or profit) there is no category for housewives, for instance. Present members of the Armed Forces were estimated independently for the earlier years, although it was not possible to make distinctions by military rank. The unemployed were omitted from the list because even those who had work experience encompassed a broad range of occupations.

How to Use the Occupational Status Scores

There are basically two ways in which these occupational scores can be used for research purposes:

First, they may be assigned to occupational categories reported in the census for analyzing census data themselves. This can be done either by using already-published cross-tabulations of occupations and other variables or by tabulating data anew from census public-use sample data sets. The occupational status scores devised by us for 1950 were, in fact, entered along with other socioeconomic information on the basic census records in 1960. Analysts using the 1960 Census public-use sample records thus have ready access to those data. They were not placed on the 1970 Census records, however.

Second, these occupational scores may be assigned on the basis of data gathered by individual researchers or agencies. For example, an individual may be conducting an original survey in which reports on occupation are crucial to the analysis. Or a social service agency may want to characterize the occupational status of each client in order to better interpret the social circumstances surrounding the clients' cases. Or a governmental agency may want to code occupational data included on public records, such as vital statistics, employment records, or health forms, in order to compare the distributions for the populations covered with specific regional or local population standards. These status scores may, therefore, have application in business, industry, government, universities—the private or public sector--or wherever a determination of socioeconomic status is desired and occupational information is available.

The actual procedure for assigning these occupational scores can be illustrated with reference to a hypothetical small-scale survey conducted by a graduate student doing research for a thesis. Let us suppose that the student has undertaken a study in the early 1970's of the dietary habits of a random sample of 250 residents of a middle-size community. Included in the interview schedule was a question asking for the occupation engaged in by the head of the household, and this is to be used as an index of the household's socioeconomic status. Let us further suppose that three-fourths of the household heads designated were men and one-fourth women.

The student would first turn to Table A1 in the Appendix of this volume and select the appropriate column in that table. In this case, the "Total" column which includes both sexes might be the optimum one. The next task would be to translate the reported occupational information for each individual into a census detailed occupational category. This can best be achieved by going through an intermediate step of locating the occupation as reported in the survey in *Alphabetical Index of Industries and Occupations* (U.S. Bureau of the Census, 1971), which should be located in any major library or can be purchased from the U.S. Government Printing Office. Thus, a "playwright" is coded 181 which is included under the detailed occupational category "Authors." A "typewriter serviceman" is coded 484 and included under "Office machine mechanics and repairmen." If the entry for occupation were "Flyer," however, one would want to know the business or industry in which it was practiced. If it was in an agricultural field, it would be coded 163 for "Airline pilot," whereas if it was in a textile field, it would be coded 674 for "Textile operative." The third step would be to find the detailed occupation in the appropriate part of the table and then transcribe the status score for that occupation.

In the event that the occupational report in the student's survey cannot be located in the *Alphabetical Index of Industries and Occupations*, an attempt should be made to find similar titles in the list. A general dictionary may be helpful in this regard. If no match of an occupation can be made, it will be necessary to approximate the occupational classification on some other basis or discard the case for purposes of the occupational analysis. This should not occur very often.

Once the occupations are identified in the census list and the associated scores determined, analysis of the data can proceed. At this stage, it is sometimes necessary to collapse the status scores to a limited number of intervals or categories before tabulation. Since the status scores developed here form a continuous distribution between 0 and 100, the selection of cutting points for defining intervals is somewhat arbitrary. One might delineate deciles or quartiles of the scores (e.g., 0-9, 10-19, etc., or 0-24, 25-49, etc.). A generally preferable alternative is to array the scores for persons in the study sample and examine the array for "natural breaks" in the distribution. The selection of group intervals can then be made in such a way that clusters of scores will not be subdivided into different intervals and the "natural groupings" thereby disturbed. The continuous nature of the scores also means that there is no meaningful way to designate any interval of scores as standing for "upper class," "middle class," "lower class," or similar terminology. Any labels attached to groups of scores will be done as a matter of convenience to the analyst.

Examples of Occupational Status Score Use

There are numerous examples in the research literature of the use of these occupational status scores. Discussed below are several illustrations of their use in a variety of research situations:

1. Karabel and Astin (1975) analyzed the relative influence of social background and academic ability in determining the quality of the college a person attended. Social class was measured by the authors' own composite index which incorporated the Nam-Powers occupational score. Academic ability was found to be the more powerful predictor of quality of college attended, but social class also had an independent effect.

2. Osmond and Schrader (1979) examined correlates of poverty among welfare applicants/clients in four states of the United States. Current employment patterns and occupational status (as measured by the Nam-Powers index) were the structural variables most highly correlated with total gross family income (the poverty indicator). Independent of occupational status and other structural variables, the female-headed family emerged as the most economically disadvantaged family unit.

3. Martin (1979) studied 23 halfway houses for alcoholics to determine factors related to staff expectations that residents would behave independently. The percentage of residents employed and their mean weekly earnings were positively related to staff expectations. Although mean occupational status (measured by Nam-Powers scores) varied from 26 to 81 (out of a range from 0 to 100) among the houses, status was not correlated with staff expectations.

4. Lehr *et al.* (1973) attempted to develop a predictive model of coronary-prone individuals. Simultaneous examination was made of social precursors (including occupational status of patients and their

fathers as indexed by the Nam-Powers measure) and standard risk or biological factors in relation to clinically-manifest coronary heart disease. Both sets of factors were found to be useful explanatory factors.

5. Dominguez and Page (1981) surveyed a range of consumer behavior research and concluded that business researchers were often not correct in their use of social stratification variables. A distinction needs to be made between class, which centers on the individual and his/her occupation, and status, which revolves around the family and its position in the community. Class is best suited to measuring those values, lifestyles, and communication patterns that are centered on work, leisure, investment, saving, and attitudes toward and perceptions of financial outlook. The Nam-Powers index is cited as the preferred class scale. In their analysis of banking values and banking behavior of the public, the authors discover that what distinguishes the banking values of the elite market segment is their income level, while what distinguishes their banking behavior is their class position. Lower social strata are found to be interested in banking behavior but are not catered to adequately by banking interests.

6. Udry *et al.* (1975) employ the Nam-Powers index as a control variable in studying the premarital coital experience of different birth cohorts of women. They found that coital experience increased over time and this trend was independent of the occupational status distribution of women which had been shifting upward.

7. Cooney *et al.* (1980) wanted to study sexual inequality in the labor force. Earlier studies comparing the occupational status of men and women were flawed, they believed, because the status indicator (Duncan's SEI) was standardized on men only. Using the Nam-Powers scores for both sexes combined, the authors concluded that women have made small but consistent progress on occupational status but have not been able to translate such gains into improved earnings relative to men's earnings. These findings are at variance with the earlier studies.

8. Udry, in another piece of research (1977), was interested in finding out the relative importance of feminine attractiveness and higher education as a vehicle for upward mobility through marriage. Mobility was measured as the difference in Nam-Powers occupational scores for the woman's father and her husband. Education was the stronger predictor for white women, whereas education and attractiveness were equally good predictors for black women.

REFERENCES

Coleman, Richard and Lee Rainwater. 1978. *Social Standing in America: New Dimensions of Class.* New York: Basic Books.

Cooney, Rosemary S., Alice S. Clague and Joseph J. Salvo. 1980. "Multiple Dimensions of Sexual Inequality in the Labor Force: 1970-1977." *Review of Public Data Use* 8: 279-293.

Dominguez, Luis V. and Albert L. Page. 1981. "Use and Misuse of Social Stratification in Consumer Behavior Research." *Journal of Business Research* 9: 151-173.

Duncan, Otis D. 1961. "A Socioeconomic Index for All Occupations." In Albert J. Reiss, Jr., *et al. Occupations and Social Status.* New York: Free Press, pp. 109-138.

Edwards, Alba M. 1943. *Comparative Occupation Statistics for the United States, 1870 to 1940.* Sixteenth Census of the United States, 1940, Population. Washington, DC: U.S. Government Printing Office.

Garbin, Albeno P. and Frederick L. Bates. 1961. "Occupational Prestige: An Empirical Study of its Correlates." *Social Forces* 40: 131-136.

Karabel, Jerome and Alexander W. Astin. 1975. "Social Class, Academic Ability, and College 'Quality'." *Social Forces* 53: 381-398.

Lehr, Irene, Harley B. Messinger and Ray H. Rosenman. 1973. "A Sociological Approach to the Study of Coronary Heart Disease." *Journal of Chronic Disease* 26: 13-30.

Martin, Patricia Y. 1979. "Client's Characteristics and the Expectations of Staff in Halfway Houses for Alcoholics." *Journal of Studies on Alcohol* 40: 211-221.

Miller, Ann R., *et al.*, eds. 1980. *Work, Jobs, and Occupations; A Critical Review of the Dictionary of Occupational Titles.* Washington, DC: National Academy Press.

Nam, Charles B., John LaRocque, Mary G. Powers and Joan Holmberg. 1975. "Occupational Status Scores: Stability and Change." *Proceedings of the American Statistical Association, Social Statistics Section,* pp. 570-575.

Nam, Charles B. and Mary G. Powers. 1968. "Changes in the Relative Status Level of Workers in the United States, 1950-1960." *Social Forces* 47: 158-170.

Osmond, Marie W. and David F. Schrader. 1979. "Paths to Poverty in the United States." *International Review of Modern Sociology* 9: 77-91.

Pavalko, Ronald M. 1971. *Sociology of Occupations and Professions.* Itasca, IL: Peacock, p. 112.

Powers, Mary G. and Joan J. Holmberg. 1978. "Occupational Status Scores: Changes Introduced by the Inclusion of Women." *Demography* 15: 183-204.

Reiss, Albert J., Jr. 1961. *Occupations and Social Status.* New York: Free Press, pp. 83-84.

Treas, Judith and Andrea Tyree. 1971. "Prestige Versus Socioeconomic Status in the Attainment Processes of American Men and Women." *Social Science Research* 8: 201-221.

Udry, J. Richard. 1977. "The Importance of Being Beautiful: A Reexamination and Racial Comparison." *American Journal of Sociology* 83: 154-160.

Udry, J. Richard, Karl E. Bauman and Naomi M. Morris. 1975. "Changes in Premarital Coital Experience of Recent Decade-of-Birth Cohorts of Women." *Journal of Marriage and the Family* 37: 783-787.

U.S. Bureau of the Census. 1963. *Methodology and Scores of Socioeconomic Status.* Working Paper No. 15. Washington, DC: U.S. Bureau of the Census.

U.S. Bureau of the Census. 1980a. *1980 Census of Population, Classified Index of Industries and Occupations.* Washington, DC: U.S. Government Printing Office.

U.S. Bureau of the Census. 1980b. *1980 Census of Population, Alphabetical Index of Industries and Occupations.* Washington, DC: U.S. Government Printing Office.

U.S. Department of Commerce. 1980. *Standard Occupational Classificational Manual.* Washington, DC: U.S. Government Printing Office.

U.S. Department of Labor. 1965. *Dictionary of Occupational Titles.* Third Edition.

Washington, DC: US. Government Printing Office.
U.S. Department of Labor. 1977. *Dictionary of Occupational Titles.* Fourth Edition. Washington, DC: U.S. Government Printing Office.

4
Socioeconomic Status and Status Consistency

Although single-item indicators of socioeconomic status are frequently preferred for reasons of ease in estimating status and simplicity of interpretation, a variety of multiple-item indicators of socioeconomic status can be found in the research literature.

At least three arguments can be advanced for a multiple-item approach. First, if there is interest in accounting for the socioeconomic status levels of individuals or groups, an attempt should be made to explain as much of the general status variable as possible. Additional items will usually add to the explanation of variance in status. Second, even though one item (e.g., occupation) may account for more of the phenomenon we call status than other items, it is likely that different items will tap somewhat different dimensions of socioeconomic status and together will more fully represent overall socioeconomic status. Third, if status is measured in terms of a combination of dimensions, the extent to which these various indicators describe status in the same way or differently can be examined. That is, their consistency or inconsistency in this respect will provide additional information about status patterns.

Some Multiple-Item Measures of Socioeconomic Status

There are several well-known socioeconomic measures which are based on more than one item. Three of them, which use different numbers and kinds of terms, are Hollingshead's Two-Factor Index of Social Position, Warner *et al.*'s Index of Status Characteristics, and Kiser and Whelpton's Summary Index of Socio-Economic Status. These were discussed briefly in Chapter 1 but are elaborated on below.

Hollingshead's Two-Factor Index is composed of an occupational scale and an educational scale (Miller, 1977, 230-238; Hollingshead and Redlich, 1958). (A variant of this socioeconomic measure also includes a residential area scale.) Occupations are classified on a seven-point scale which takes account of the Edwards' occupational grouping but differentiates among types of professionals and divides business and farm jobs by the size and value of the establishment. Thus, the occupational categories are Higher Executives of Large Concerns, Proprietors of Medium-Sized Businesses, and Lesser Professionals; Administrative Personnel, Owners of Small Businesses, and Minor Professionals; Clerical and Sales Workers, Technicians, and Owners of Little Businesses; Skilled Manual Employees; Machine Operators and Semi-skilled Employees; and Unskilled Employees.

There are also seven categories in the educational scale: Graduate Professional Training; Standard College or University Graduation; Partial College Training; High School Graduation; Partial High School; Junior High School; and less than Seven Years of School.

In each scale, the highest status is assigned the value 7 and the lowest the value 1. In order to arrive at the total index, the occupation value is weighted by 7 and the educational value is weighted by 4. The sum of the weighted values gives the Index of Social Position Score, which can range from 11 to 77.

Although occupation and education are obviously correlated to some degree, they each contribute a certain amount of independent explanation of overall status. By combining the two indicators, more variance in status can be accounted for.

Warner, Meeker, and Eells devised an Index of Status Characteristics (I.S.C.) for their analysis of class structure in Yankee City and other communities (Miller, 1977, 239-243; Warner, Meeker, and Eells, 1949). This index is composed of four variables—occupation, source of income, house type, and dwelling area. There are parallels between this measure and Hollingshead's in that each item is rated on a seven-point scale and the total index is based on a weighted combination of the scores for the four items. The occupational component categorizes jobs in a manner similar to that of Hollingshead and would appear to have been a forerunner of the latter, although this is a controversial issue. The source of income dimension differentiates among chief sources such as inherited wealth, earned wealth, profits and fees, salary, wages, private relief, and public relief and nonrespectable income. House type is classified according to excellent, very good, good, average, fair, poor, and very poor, based on interviewer examination of size, style, and condition. The classification of dwelling areas used interviewers'ratings of general appearance of areas as being very high, high, above average, average, below average, low, and very low.

Weights assigned to the four item values were calculated from a multiple-regression equation which employed a family's reputation as a criterion of status. On this basis, occupation received a weight of 4, source of income and house type got weights of 3 each, and dwelling area earned a weight of 2. The total index score is a weighted sum of the component item values. The composite score could take values from 12 to 84.

Socioeconomic measures can incorporate even more items, as evidenced by Kiser and Whelpton's (1949) Index of Socio-Economic Status. This index was composed of eight items, including husband's average annual earnings since marriage, net worth, shelter rent at interview, husband's longest occupational class since marriage, purchase price of car, education of husband, education of wife, and rating of the household on Chapin's Social Status Scale. Scores ranging from 0 (high) to 9 (low) were assigned for each item and the several scores were summed to produce a composite rating which could take values from 1 to 72. Couples sampled for the famous Indianapolis Study of Social and Psychological Factors Affecting Fertility were classified by this index and the scores were related to family planning status and size of family. The authors concluded that the multiple-item index seemed to account for considerably more variation in fertility behavior than any individual or smaller group of items.

U.S. Census Multiple-Item Socioeconomic Measure

Persons working with census data who want to use an indicator of socioeconomic status are restricted to what can be derived from census items. As indicated in Chapter 2, a variety of indicators has been included in the several censuses. Among these, occupation has received the greatest attention, but education, income, and housing characteristics also lend themselves to socioeconomic classification.

Alba Edward's occupational categorization received widespread use by social researchers but was acknowledged to have a number of methodological shortcomings. The newer occupational status variable, based on the median education and income of occupational incumbents, overcame several of those shortcomings and represented a valuable socioeconomic, as opposed to prestige, dimension of status. The resulting occupational scores also can be interpreted in a straightforward manner as indicating the percentage of workers having lower status than the average person in the given occupation. (See Chapter 3.)

While this occupational index is an improvement over earlier ones, the fact remains that it is concerned with only a single item which does not capture all of the variation in socioeconomic status. This is mainly because the score relates to the occupational aggregate or the average person in an occupation, and there still remains variation around that average. Within any occupation, there are persons who have more or less education and income which may be associated with different levels of responsibility and performance in that occupation.

Acknowledging that an occupational measure by itself will often be most appropriate for particular analyses because of the nature of available data and the purpose of the analysis, there was interest in extending socioeconomic measurement to permit more complete analysis. In addition, there was a desire to have more elaborate tools of socioeconomic analysis for application to the census data themselves. As a result, a multiple-item approach was devised which used indicators of occupation, education, and income for key persons in each family and assigned resulting scores to each family member (Nam *et al.*, 1963).

Several considerations had to be made in the choice of items to be included, how they were to be rated and combined, and various other statistical procedures to be followed.

A basic assumption in the construction of the multiple-item socioeconomic measure was that the status level of a family is indexed largely by status attributes of the main family breadwinner and, thus, that the socioeconomic indicators for the chief income recipient of a family should be assigned to other family members. This principal person may be male or female and there may be more than one earner in the family, but the chief income recipient's characteristics will be indicative of the family's status. (The increase in dual-worker families and the possible different characteristics of the two or more workers challenges this critical assumption, but this assumption is supportable when family income is included in the computation. For further discussion and evaluation of this point, see Chapter 5.)

The chief income recipient in a family was defined as that member of a family who had the largest total income (at least $1 more than any other family member). If the family head and one or more other family members had identical incomes and they had the highest incomes in the family or if no family member had reported income, the family head was considered the chief income recipient. If two or more family members other than the head had equal and highest incomes, the first one listed was regarded as the chief income recipient.

Each unrelated individual 14 years old or over, in households, and each person in group quarters (including inmates of institutions, members of the Armed Forces in military barracks, students in college dormitories, and residents in rooming houses) was treated as a chief income recipient.

The measures for chief income recipients in families were assigned to other family members. Since a child under 14 cannot reasonably be regarded as having a socioeconomic status independent of that of the household in which he or she lives, unrelated individuals under 14 in households (mostly foster children) were assigned the same scores as the head of the households, on the assumption that such children generally share the living conditions of the household head. In order to complete the assignment of scores for all persons, those under 14 years old in group quarters were also assigned no school years completed.

The component items of the measures (occupation, education, and income) were selected because they represent different aspects of socioeconomic status and, in addition, because they are items on which information is regularly collected through the Census Bureau's censuses and surveys as well as other data sources. A housing item (e.g., rent or value of home) was not included because relevant housing information is not obtained regularly in Census Bureau or other inquiries. An ethnic characteristic (e.g., race or nationality) was not included because it was felt that such an item can be more properly treated as a correlate of, rather than as a component of, socioeconomic status.

The choice of a particular index of each component item was based, in part, on the kinds of data available in census reports and, in part, on the expected uses to which the socioeconomic data would be put. Family income (or income of unrelated individuals outside of families) rather than the income of the chief income recipient, was initially chosen because it was determined that the socioeconomic status of a family was related more closely to the family income than to the income of the chief earner. Multiple earners, for example, permit the purchase of more consumption goods. In the process of developing the family income scores, the effect of measuring family income in different ways (simple family income, per capita family income, and family income adjusted for differences in the composition of the family) was studied. The available data showed that the effect of the adjustments on a person's socioeconomic score was generally minor, and this fact argued for maintaining the simple measure of family income. Beginning with the 1980 Census, changes in family and household concepts rendered "household income" as most comparable to the previous concept of "family and unrelated individual income" which, in fact, was used in the earlier measurement approach.

The occupation, if any, for a chief income recipient was used, provided that person was currently in the civilian labor force or, if not, had worked during the previous ten years. Since the rank and duties of members of the Armed Forces are not known from the census, chief income recipients currently in the Armed Forces were assigned a uniform occupational rating. For a chief income recipient without an occupation reported, his or her score on education was assigned as the score for occupation as well.

(a)The scores for education were obtained by computing a cumulative percentage distribution by educational attainment for chief income recipients in families as of a date close to the census period. (For example, persons who had completed five or more years of college were found to be distributed between the 96th and 100th percentiles.) The score assigned to each category of education was the midpoint of the cumulative percentage interval for that category. (For example, a score of 98 was assigned to persons who had completed five or more years of college.)

(b)The scores for family income were obtained in a similar manner by assigning midpoints of cumulative percentage intervals to each family income category.

(c)The scores for detailed occupations were based on the most recently available data. The occupations were scored according to the combined average levels of education and income for the given occupation. The scores thus obtained are for the average person in an occupational category. As in the cases of the education and family income scores, the occupational score is a midpoint of the cumulative percentage interval for an occupation ranked by average education and income of its incumbents. The occupational score is thus independent of the education and income scores for individuals.

The multiple-item socioeconomic status score was determined in the following way: (a) The occupation, education, and family income for each chief income recipient were identified, (b) using the scores computed for each component, appropriate scores for each chief income recipients item characteristics were located, (c) a simple average of the three component scores was calculated, and (d) the result was rounded to the nearest whole score.

It would have been possible to "build in" to the scores for items, or the summary socioeconomic measures, adjustments for differences among socioeconoimic groups in age, residence, and other demographic characteristics. This was not done because it was felt that often these items would be the subjects of socioeconomic analysis and, where it was deemed important for other types of analysis, the desired adjustments could be made in the tabulation process.

It was pointed out that the combination of the three component items into the summary measure was on the basis of simple averaging of the three scores. Consideration was given to differential weighting of the component items; however, at the time this measure was developed, there was no adequate basis for establishing weights through internal factorial analysis. Moreover, there is no independent criterion of status against which these scores can be regressed.

Another way of viewing the multiple-item approach being used is to say that the education and family income scores help in refining the occupational score by accounting for some of the variation in status among individuals within the same occupational category.

It should be noted that the scores for each of the component items are distributed so that about 10 per cent of the persons in the population fall in each tenth of the distribution of the item. In the case of the summary socioeconomic scores, however, larger percentages of persons are generally found in the central part of the distribution and smaller percentages are at the extremes.

Some Approaches to Measuring Status Consistency

An objection sometimes raised with regard to the derivation of multiple-item socioeconomic indexes is that the components of such indexes not only are frequently of a different sort but also each may place the subject being studied at different status levels. A response to such an objection is that (a) socioeconomic status is basically an attribute of individuals which is broader in concept than any one measurable characteristic and a multiple-item approach can, therefore, more closely approximate the attribute, and (b) the extent of similarity or dissimilarity of two or more indicators of status in itself is a meaningful aspect of one's socioeconomic profile and analytically separate from the overall status level.

The notion of status inconsistency is well established in the social science literature. It is used to refer to disparities among statuses in varying situations (e.g., characteristics of different groups or aggregates, characteristics of different individuals, or different characteristics of the same individual) (Kasl, 1969).

Perhaps the most widely-cited methodological approach to status inconsistency measurement is that of Lenski (1954). He chose four variables (education, occupation, income, and racial-ethnic status) for comparison. Ratings on each of these variables were converted into normalized percentile scores. A mean status score was computed and an index of "status incongruence" derived by taking the square root of the sums of squared deviations of each item score from the mean and subtracting it from 100. The several variables were weighted equally and no identification of types of status incongruence was made.

Lenski's approach, or variants of it, have been used in a number of studies designed to get at the effects of status inconsistency on various forms of social behavior. Critics of Lenski's work have pointed to the importance of the component variables selected and the fact that racial-ethnic status, different in kind from the other status variables, is often a discrepant component. Others have argued that status inconsistency may be an expected temporary condition which reflects a life-cycle stage and controls need to established for that structural effect. Nevertheless, the use of status consistency-inconsistency measures persists.

Nam-Powers Status Inconsistency Approach

When the multiple-item socioeconomic scoring system was being devised, we had in mind the opportunity to measure status consistency-inconsistency patterns as well. For reasons cited above, having an overall socioeconomic measure in combination with a consistency type would provide us with especially powerful tools for analyzing census data.

It was also apparent to us that both socioeconomic status and status consistency were relative measures which were to be used in comparative analysis. Reckoning absolute levels of the two phenomena was not possible or particularly desirable. What was important was the meaningfulness of the measures and the distribution of values which were generated.

We experimented with alternatives in items used and statistical criteria as well. For example, just as we tested for the effect of using family income *vis-a-vis* other income measures in the multiple-item socioeconomic score, we examined the effect of family income vs. other income measures in regard to the status consistency construct. Because the variation in outcome was so slight, we selected the items and procedures which seemed to us most optimum for the two measures.

The fundamental approach in generating the status consistency type was to compare the percentile scores for the three component items of the overall SES measure. Determination of consistency or inconsistency, and the nature of inconsistency, was based on a discrepancy of 20 or fewer percentile points between pairs of items. This level of discrepancy was chosen, after inspection of sample data showing variations in distributions, as representing a critical dividing line.

Thirteen status consistency types were derived, which may be described as follows:

Figure 4-1: Status Consistency Typology

Status Consistency Type:	Characteristics:
1	All three components consistent
2	Occupation and education consistent; income high
3	Occupation and education consistent; income low
4	Occupation and income consistent; education high
5	Occupation and income consistent; education low
6	Education and income consistent; occupation high
7	Education and income consistent; occupation low
8	All inconsistent; occupation highest; income lowest

9 All inconsistent; occupation highest; education lowest
10 All inconsistent; education highest; occupation lowest
11 All inconsistent; education highest; income lowest
12 All inconsistent; income highest; occupation lowest
13 All inconsistent; income highest; education lowest

The procedure which produced that typology can be elaborated as follows:

Using the percentile scores for the three component items:

a) If the range between the highest and lowest scores was 20 or less, Type 1 was assigned.

b) If the range between the highest and lowest scores exceeded 20, and the range between the medium and lowest scores was 20 or less and less than the range between the highest and medium scores, then

i) Type 2 was assigned if the income scores was highest
ii) Type 4 was assigned if the education score was highest
iii) Type 6 was assigned if the occupation score was highest.

c) If the range between the highest and lowest scores exceeded 20, and the range between the highest and medium scores was 20 or less and equal to or less than the range between the medium and lowest scores, then

i) Type 3 was assigned if the income score was lowest
ii) Type 5 was assigned if the education score was lowest
iii) Type 7 was assigned if the occupation score was lowest.

d) If the range between the highest and medium scores and the medium and lowest scores each exceed 20, then

i) Type 8 was assigned if the occupation was highest and income score lowest

ii) Type 9 was assigned if the occupation score was highest and education score lowest

iii) Type 10 was assigned if the education score was highest and occupation score lowest

iv) Type 11 was assigned if the education score was highest and income score lowest

v) Type 12 was assigned if the income score was highest and occupation score lowest

vi) Type 13 was assigned if the income score was highest and education score lowest.

Using the Census Socioeconomic Measures

One advantage of the measures developed here is that they provide national norms for socioeconomic status and status consistency. As a consequence, they offer a basis for comparison of distributions from smaller samples or for population subgroups. It is necessary, however, that data being compared refer to the same date.

Occupational percentile scores were referred to in Chapter 3 and are shown in the Appendix for different population groups. The percentile scores for education and household income are shown for 1980 in the Appendices as well. If the multiple-item socioeconomic scores and status consistency types are to be calculated for other dates, it will be necessary to acquire standard percentile distributions for education and family or household income for approximately those dates in order to have standards from which to compute the measures.

Some Properties of the Socioeconomic Measures

A description of variations in the measures by race, residence, and age for the United States (Nam and Powers, 1965) should suffice to indicate some of the properties of the two multiple-item measures and the utility of the measures for social research.

The multiple-item socioeconomic indicator (SES) distribution for family heads by race and residence in 1960 is depicted in Figure 1. Since the distribution for all family heads combined is essentially normal, with a slight skewness toward the lower levels, group differences in socioeconomic status can be viewed graphically in terms of departures from a normal distribution.

For both white and nonwhite family heads, a more favorable socioeconomic distribution was found in the central cities and urban fringes of these cities than outside urbanized areas (that is, in rural areas and small towns and cities). Concentration in the lowest third of the SES range was especially marked among nonwhite family heads residing outside urbanized areas, but the proportion of nonwhite family heads in the highest SES level was also larger outside than inside urbanized areas. Although there was virtually no nonwhite middle class in these areas, a small nonwhite elite did exist, probably consisting of professional and business people serving the nonwhite population, especially in segregated communities.

Other data, not shown in the figure, reveal that persons in urban places outside urbanized areas, like those in central cities, had status distributions much like the total populations. In contrast, the status disadvantages of the rural population, particularly the rural-farm population, were striking. Whereas 39 per cent of urban fringe residents had SES scores of 70 or higher, only 6 per cent of the rural-farm

Figure 4-1. Socioeconomic Status of Family Heads by Race and Residence: 1960

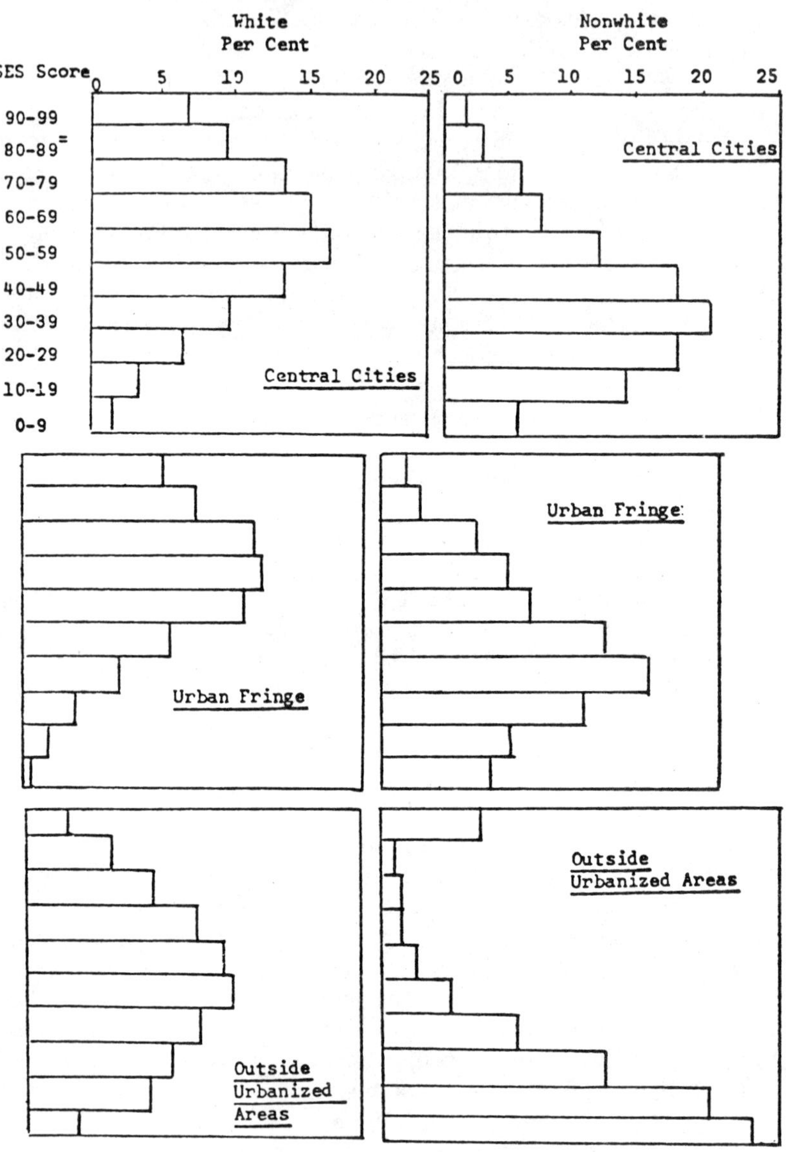

Source: Nam and Powers. 1965. See References.

population had such high scores. Only 8 per cent of persons in the urban fringe had scores below 30, compared with 49 per cent of the farm population, and half of the nonwhites on farms had scores below 10. The distribution of whites in farm areas was similar to that of nonwhites in central cities. (The other data referred to in this paragraph were for the total population rather than for family heads, but the socioeconomic distributions for these two universes are very similar.)

Table 4-1 shows patterns of status consistency for white and nonwhite family heads 35 to 54 years old in various residence areas. By limiting the data to family heads of prime working ages, we have minimized the influence of the irregular status pattern displayed by many younger and older family heads. Consistent and inconsistent types, grouped by extent of inconsistency, are shown within broad categories of Socioeconomic status to indicate the general status levels at which the consistency patterns occur. Since the patterns obtained are, in part, a function of the procedures used, greater emphasis should be placed on using these data for comparative analysis than on determining absolute levels of SES and consistency in different groups. (The method used to measure status consistency results in about 30 per cent of all family heads having consistent statuses.)

As expected, the proportion of persons with consistent statuses was greatest at the lowest and highest SES levels in every group, and inconsistency was characteristic of the middle socioeconomic ranges. Variations in consistency distributions among racial and residence groups were generally small, but there were some notable deviations from the general pattern.

Among family heads with status scores of 80 or higher, the percentage with consistent statuses was slightly higher for nonwhites than for whites in urbanized areas but much lower for nonwhites than whites outside urbanized areas. These differences may be partly a function of the dissimilarity of SES distributions by race even within the top status range and of the small, and hence statistically less reliable, sample of nonwhites at this socioeconomic level.

Nonwhite family heads with SES scores of 50 to 79 who did not live in large cities were somewhat less likely than whites to have consistent statuses. Detailed data by consistency type reveal that unequal opportunities for nonwhites to achieve jobs and income commensurate with their education characterized all areas but particularly areas outside central cities. For family heads with scores of 20 to 49, broad consistency patterns among color and residence groups were more similar than in the upper part of the middle SES range, but the economic disadvantage of nonwhites could still be observed. Among family heads at the lowest status levels, consistency differentials by color

Table 4-1. Status Consistency of Family Heads Ages 35 to 54, by Race, Residence, and Socioeconomic Status: 1960 (in percentages)*

Socioeconomic status and consistency type	White family heads: Central cities	White family heads: Urban fringe	White family heads: Outside urbanized areas	Nonwhite family heads: Central cities	Nonwhite family heads: Urban fringe	Nonwhite family heads: Outside urbanized areas
All SES scores	(5,575)	(4,733)	(8,493)	(1,096)	(187)	(704)
	100	100	100	100	100	100
All status consistent	28	31	28	26	25	46
One status inconsistent	62	59	63	63	65	50
All statuses inconsistent	11	10	9	11	11	4
SES scores 80 to 99 (high)	(1,118)	(1,289)	(1,040)	(47)	(10)	(9)
	100	100	100	100	100	100
All status consistent	64	64	61	68	70	22
One status inconsistent	36	36	39	32	30	78
All statuses inconsistent**	--	--	--	--	--	--
SES scores 50 to 79	(2,834)	(2,551)	(3,474)	(271)	(49)	(52)
	100	100	100	100	100	100
All status consistent	19	21	21	19	16	10
One status inconsistent	68	67	68	70	74	83
All statuses inconsistent	13	12	11	11	10	8
SES scores 20 to 49	(1,476)	(847)	(3,225)	(600)	(100)	(260)
	100	100	100	100	100	100
All statuses consistent	12	11	14	15	13	11
One status inconsistent	72	72	75	70	72	79
All statuses inconsistent	16	17	11	15	15	10
SES scores 0 to 19 (low)	(147)	(46)	(754)	(178)	(28)	(383)
	100	100	100	100	100	100
All statuses consistent	61	57	73	61	64	76
One status inconsistent	39	44	27	39	36	25
All statuses inconsistent**	--	--	--	--	--	--

*Number of sample cases is shown in parentheses.

**The criterion for consistency makes it impossible for persons with extreme SES status scores to have all statuses inconsistent.

Source: Nam and Powers, 1965. (See References.)

were moderate but those by residence were sharply drawn.

By combining SES and consistency data, we can learn more about particular status groups in our society. For example, abject poverty is not based on low income alone. Individuals who also rank low on occupation and education lack the potential for mobility. Three-fourths of the family heads 35 to 54 years old with SES scores under 20 who were living outside urbanized areas ranked low in all three status hierarchies, compared with three-fifths of those in urbanized areas (Table 4-1). Among all nonwhite family heads outside urbanized areas,

41 per cent had consistently low statuses, compared to 10 per cent of nonwhites in urbanized areas, 7 per cent of whites outside urbanized areas, and 1 per cent of whites in urbanized areas. Data for the farm population indicate that about 20 per cent of white family heads and about 60 per cent of nonwhite family heads had consistently low statuses.

Families in an impoverished condition, as indexed by low status in all three hierarchies, numbered three and one-half million in 1960; one million of these were nonwhite. Other census data indicate that the total number of families with incomes of less than $3,000 was about nine and one-half million, of whom two million were nonwhite. Thus, about one-third of the white families who would be regarded as poor on the basis of income alone were also of low education and occupational status, whereas this proportion was one-half for nonwhites.

Variations in socioeconomic level throughout the life cycle can be described in terms of age. Family heads under 25 years of age had a fairly normal SES distribution with a concentration at the center. At ages 25 to 34, the distribution shifted toward the higher status levels, so that the modal status was in the 50-59 score range. Family heads 35 to 44 years old had still a higher average SES level and a much more platykurtic distribution than the younger groups. Among family heads 45 to 54, the average socioeconomic level was lower and the distribution again approached normality with a slight bias toward high scores. (Our tabulations do not indicate the specific age at which the decline begins.) The reversal continued among those 55 to 64 years old, with the modal status in the 40-49 range. Status levels among the oldest family heads, those 65 and older were extremely low, with the modal score in the 10-19 range.

The attainment of peak status in education, occupation, and income occurs at different times in the life span of the average individual. Ordinarily, one's formal education is completed at an early age, at least before age 35; the type of occupation in which a person settles may have been entered at an early age but usually is not clearly determined until formal education has been completed; and peak earnings are usually not achieved, nor is family income at its highest, until some years of employment have passed. Of course, subgroups of the population vary in timing of these events. For these reasons, the point in the life cycle at which persons are evaluated decidedly affects their socioeconomic position.

The diagrams in Figure 4-2 describe status levels and consistency patterns for family heads in six consecutive age groups. The eleven possible categories of inconsistency have been grouped differently here than they were in Table 4-1 where the distinctions was based on the number of inconsistent status components. In Figure 4-2, inconsistency is defined in terms of the expected

Figure 4-2. Socioeconomic Status and Status Consistency of Family Heads, by Age: 1960

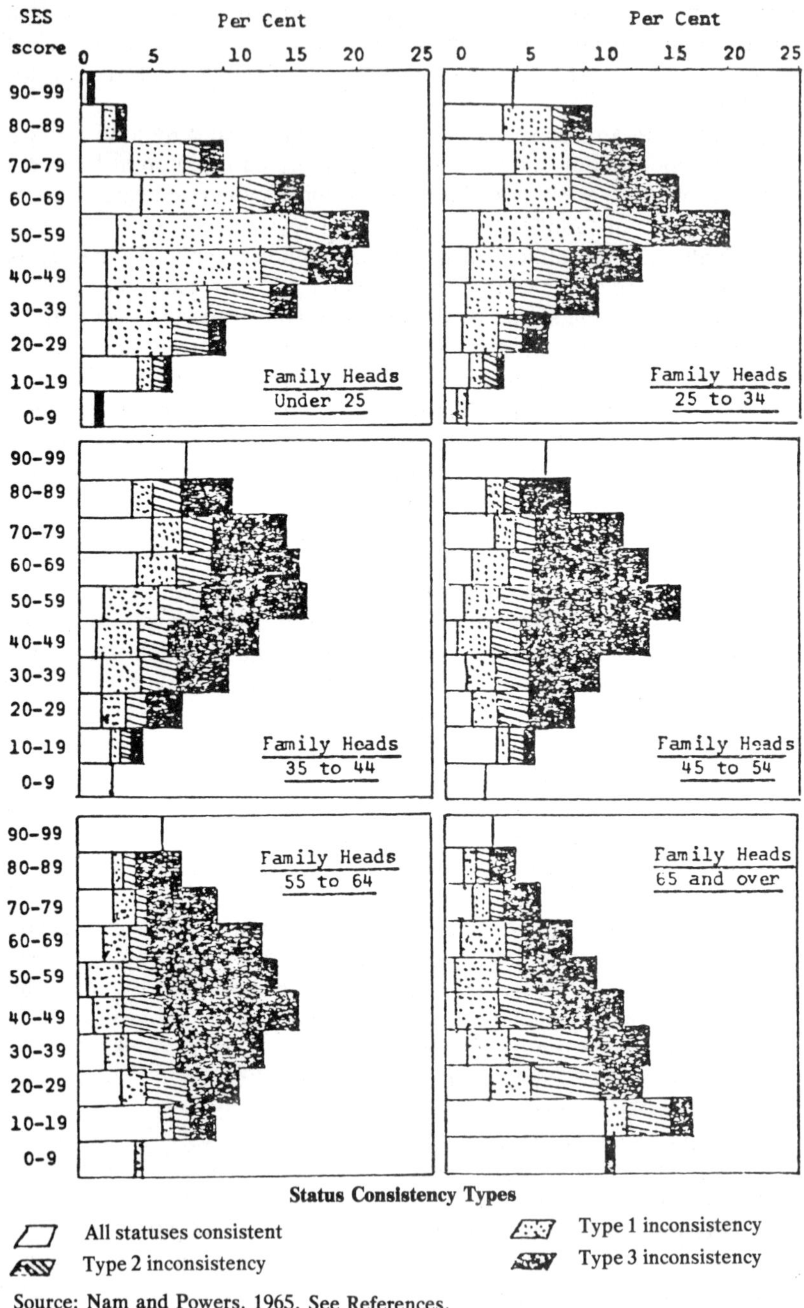

Source: Nam and Powers. 1965. See References.

education-occupation-income sequence of attained status. Type 1 inconsistency includes categories 3, 4, and 11; Type 2 inconsistency encompasses categories 6, 7, 8, and 10; and Type 3 inconsistency includes categories 2, 5, 9, and 12.

"Type 1 inconsistency" patterns could conceivably stem from a time-lag in the attainment of peak statuses. Thus, occupation and income are at lower levels than education, as is often the case for recent college graduates. In "Type 2 inconsistency," none of the statuses is more than one step out of line from the sequential pattern. For example, occupation may be higher than education, which is higher than income, for such persons as self-appointed ministers and preachers. Finally, "Type 3 inconsistency" includes patterns in which a status is two steps out of line. For instance, education may be lower than income which in turn is lower than occupation, as for older retail store proprietors.

Since Type 1 inconsistency includes persons in the process of attaining their peak statuses, it was, of course, inversely related to age. This type of inconsistency is typical of family heads uner 35 years old, most of whom have completed their education but are still gaining in economic status. Because Type 1 inconsistency is normal for persons under 35, they are not likely to view such a situation as unfavorable but, for older persons with similar inconsistencies, the situation is less normal and less likely to be temporary. Consequently, behavior patterns associated with different types of status inconsistency can be expected to vary with age.

Type 2 inconsistency showed no pronounced change with age, although it did tend to be higher in the 20-49 SES score range. Type 3 inconsistency, at each status level, increased with age until age 65, at which point it began to decline. The trend in this abnormal type of inconsistency is partly a function of historical changes in the societal level of education and occupation. The index used to measure inconsistency was based on standards for a population covering all adult ages; middle-aged and older family heads tend to have less education and, to some extent, lower occupational status, than the youngers ones, but their income is higher. The better earning capacity of persons in the middle years, resulting from tenure, job experience, and other income-producing factors, makes the tendency toward status inconsistency all the stronger. For many aged family heads, income drops to a level more commensurate with their education, thus producing less Type 3 inconsistency in the 65-and-older age group.

Several implications for research in social stratification can be drawn from the foregoing analysis:

(1) The characteristic socioeconomic differences between whites and nonwhites and between rural and urban residents should be carefully considered—and controlled where appropriate and feasible—in any

study of the relation between socioeconomic status and other variables.

(2) Age affects the distribution of socioeconomic status because shifts in status patterns occur as persons pass through the life cycle; hence, analysis involving status variables should take account of the ages of persons in the sample.

(3) The introduction of a measure of status consistency into socioeconomic analysis helps to identify more precisely certain status groups in the society; for example, the "hard-core poor," whose education and occupational status is as low as their income. Other status groups that can be identified in the same way include "elites" (consistently high statuses) and the "normal" middle class (consistently medium SES levels).

(4) Analyses of status inconsistency should distinguish specific types of inconsistency which may have different behavioral consequences. For example, when status inconsistency is a function of the normal time-lag in attaining certain statuses, it may produce little mental stress, whereas greater stress may result from status inconsistency stemming from more permanent disadvantage in some statuses.

Examples of Multiple-Item Measure Use

A number of studies have drawn on these multiple-item measures for their inclusion of socioeconomic variables. Discussed below are several illustrations of such research:

1. Myrianthopoulos and French (1968) were involved in a Collaborative Study of Cerebral Palsy, Mental Retardation and Other Neurological and Sensory Disorders of Infancy and Childhood. The study was based on information from fourteen institutions in the United States which were geographically and socioeconomically differentiated. Research was oriented to examining events affecting parents before and during pregnancy and the possible relationship of these events to occurrence of neurological deficit in the children. In addition to clinical and laboratory data, various types of socioeconomic and other background information were obtained. A slight adaptation of the Nam-Powers SES score was used in the analysis, and the distributions for the study populations were compared with each other and with the pattern for the total population of the United States and relevant subgroups of that population.

2. Hackett and Cassem (1976) investigated the influence of socioeconomic factors on responses of patients to acute myocardial infarction. These heart-condition patients ranged in age from 29 to 80. The multiple-item SES score was used to classify patients into groupings that were related to the heart ailment and other variables in a chi-square analyses. Social class differences were observed.

3. Fendrich and Smith (1980) gathered data from a stratified sample

of former black students of a southern black university ten years after a major civil rights protest. The respondents' and fathers' SES levels were measured using the Nam-Powers composite score. They found that radicalism resulted partly from blocked opportunity and partly from political socialization. Those respondents with lower SES were among the more radical students.

4. In a study by Boggs and Galliher (1975), social status of black respondents was related to attitudes toward, and experience with, the police in a major city. The survey covered 176 adults located in households and 117 found in street situations. Street respondents scored at the lowest end of the SES distribution, based on the Nam-Powers multiple-item index. The street respondents gave more negative ratings of police service in the neighborhood. Household residents were also dissatisfied but to a lesser extent. It was found that higher social status does serve as an insulator from experiences with police and influences evaluations of police performance.

5. Broman, Nichols, and Kennedy (1975) analyzed 169 prenatal and postnatal variables and the intellectual performance at age four of 26,760 children whose mothers enrolled during pregnancy in a national project. The multiple-item SES score was one of the variables used and turned out to be the most powerful explainer of the dependent variables.

6. Chiricos and Waldo (1975) made an empirical test of the proposition that, when sanctions are imposed, the most severe sanctions will be imposed on persons in the lowest social class. They collected data for 10,488 prison inmates who had been sentenced for seventeen specific offenses in three southeastern states. Each inmate's socioeconomic status was measured using the Nam-Powers multiple-item approach. They found no significant relationship between SES and the length of prison terms assigned by the court. The relationship held up, however, when various demographic and criminological controls were introduced.

7. See (1968) was interested in reconciling some disparate findings in the research literature on the socioeconomic selectivity of metropolitan migration. Karl and Alma Taeuber (1964) found that there was no difference between the SES levels of migrants going to the ring of the SMSA and those going to the central city. Goldstein (1963) and Goldstein and Mayer (1965) discovered that migrants to the ring were of higher SES than migrants to the central city. The Taeubers measured SES in terms of education and occupation. Goldstein used income while Goldstein and Mayer used both an education-occupation composite measure and income. See analyzed metropolitan migration streams employing both the Nam-Powers multiple-item SES score and status consistency types. His results showed that the omission of income data in the Taeubers' study accounted for much of the differ-

ence in that variations by income were more relevant than variations by education or occupation. Moreover, there was a tendency for people to move into a central city while young (and when SES was only moderate and inconsistent) and to leave for the ring at an older age (when SES was somewhat higher and the socioeconomic components tending toward consistency).

REFERENCES

Boggs, Sarah L. and John F. Galliher. 1975. "Evaluating the Police: A Comparison of Black Street and Household Respondents." *Social Problems* 22: 393-406.

Broman, Sarah H., Paul L. Nichols and Wallace A. Kennedy. 1975. *Preschool IQ: Prenatal and Early Developmental Correlates.* New York: John Wiley.

Chiricos, Theodore G. and Gordon P. Waldo. 1965. "Socioeconomic Status and Criminal Sentencing: An Empirical Assessment of a Conflict Proposition." *American Sociological Review* 40: 753-772.

Fendrich, James F. and Charles U. Smith. 1980. "Black Activists: Ten Years Later." *Journal of Negro Education* 44: 3-19.

Goldstein, Sidney. 1963. "Economic Consequences of Suburbanization in Copenhagen." *American Journal of Sociology* 68: 551-564.

Goldstein, Sidney and Kurt B. Mayer. 1965. "The Impact of Migration on the Socioeconomic Structure of Cities and Suburbs." *Sociology and Social Research* 50: 5-23.

Hackett, Thomas P. and Ned H. Cassem. 1976. "White-Collar and Blue Collar Responses to Heart Attack." *Journal of Psychosomatic Research* 20: 85-95.

Hollingshead, August B. and Frederick C. Redlich. 1958. *Social Class and Mental Illness.* New York: John Wiley, pp. 387-397.

Kasl, Stanislav V. 1969. "Status Inconsistency: Some Conceptual and Methodological Considerations." In John P. Robinson, *et al., Measures of Occupational Attitudes and Occupational Characteristics.* Ann Arbor: Institute for Social Reseach, University of Michigan, pp. 377-395.

Kiser, Clyde V. and P.K. Whelpton. 1949. "Social and Psychological Factors Affecting Fertility: IX. Fertility Planning and Fertility Rates by Socio-Economic Status." *Milbank Memorial Fund Quarterly* 27: 188-244.

Lenski, Gerhard. 1954. "Status Crystallization: A Non-Vertical Dimension of Social Status." *American Sociological Review* 19: 405-413.

Miller, Delbert C. 1977. *Handbook of Research Design and Social Measurement.* Third Edition. New York: David McKay.

Myrianthopoulos, Ntinos C. and Katherine S. French. 1968. "An Application of the U.S. Bureau of the Census Socioeconomic Index to a Large, Diversified Patient Population." *Social Science and Medicine* 2: 283-299.

Nam, Charles B., Howard G. Brunsman, Paul C. Glick and Edward G. Stockwell. 1963. *Methodology and Scores of Socioeconomic Status.* Washington, DC: U.S. Bureau of the Census.

Nam, Charles B. and Mary G. Powers. 1965. "Variations in Socioeconomic Structure by Race, Residence, and the Life Cycle." *American Sociological Review* 30: 97-103.

See, Joel J. 1968. "Socioeconomic Selectivitv of Migration to Metropolitan Areas and Between Rings and Central Cities of Metropolitan Areas." *Research Reports in Social Science* 11: 18-34.

Taeuber, Karl and Alma Taeuber. 1964. "White Migration and Socioeconomic Differentials Between Cities and Suburbs." *American Sociological Review* 29: 718-729.

Warner, W. Lloyd, Marcia Meeker and Kenneth Eells. *Social Class in America.* Chicago: Science Research Associates, pp. 121-159.

5
Women in the Labor Force and Measures of Occupational Status

By 1970, it was apparent that a revised measure of occupational status must take into account not only the changed occupational classification scheme and changes in the occupational structure, but also of changes in the composition of the labor force resulting from the increased participation of women. The increased labor force participation of women and the concomitant changing composition of the work force indicated that, by 1970, the measurement of occupational status based solely on the characteristics of male incumbents was no longer valid. A measure purporting to rank the occupational hierarchy of contemporary American society could not ignore the increasing numbers of women in that hierarchy. To evaluate the effect of this increasing participation on occupational status scores, this chapter compares occupational status scores based on the characteristics of the 1970 male experienced civilian labor force with occupational status scores based on the characteristics of the 1970 total experienced civilian labor force. It also reviews labor force trends and issues and developments in stratification theory which required the modification of traditional measures of occupational status.

Women in the Labor Force

Increases in the proportion of the labor force made up of women have been recorded each decade since 1900. By 1970, women comprised 38 per cent of the total labor force in the United States or about 31 million workers (U.S. Bureau of the Census, 1973). Such growth continued throughout the 1970's; by 1975 women made up 40 per cent of the total experienced civilian labor force and by 1980 they were 42 per cent of the civilian labor force (St. Marie & Bedwerzik, 1976; U.S.D.L., 1980). Viewed from another perspective, 26 per cent of all women 16 years old and over were in the labor force in 1940 compared to 46 per cent in 1975 and 51 per cent in 1980 (*Employment and Training Report of the President*, 1976, p. 142; U.S.D.L., 1980).

Much of the research on the increased participation of women in the labor force emphasized the extent and types of female labor force participation (Sweet, 1973; Waite, 1976); the status of women (Oppenheimer, 1970, 1973; Tyree and Treas, 1974; Treiman and Terrell, 1975; and Featherman and Hauser, 1976); and the persistent earnings gap between men and women (Fuchs, 1971; Oaxaca, 1973; Sell & Johnson, 1977-78). This chapter examines the way in which the labor force participation of women affects the measurement of occupational status and, hence, the way we conceptualize such research issues as well as the findings of such research.

Several aspects of women's labor force participation affect occupational status scores. These include: a) the earnings gap between men and women and the theoretical explanations for this gap; b) the way in which women are concentrated within occupations and industries; and c) the work experience of women as full- and part-time workers and as peripheral or marginal workers.

The Earnings Gap Between Men and Women Workers

The earnings gap between fully employed men and women has been thoroughly documented and fairly constant. For example, the median earnings of fully employed women in 1972 were only about 58 per cent of the median earnings for men. In 1974, the median income for men 25 years old and over and employed full-time all year was $12,786 compared to $7,370 for women in these same categories. Again the ratio was about .58 (U.S. Bureau of the Census, 1973 and 1976). A gap existed regardless of level of education and in every major occupational group. Women fared best relative to men in professional and technical jobs and worst in sales occupations, but the picture was similar in all major occupational categories (Fuchs, 1971, pp. 10-14). More important, perhaps, the earnings gap has not narrowed and may, in fact, have widened somewhat between 1955 and 1975 (Women's Bureau, 1976:6). At the same time that employment opportunities increased, and increasing proportions of women entered the labor force, their earnings did not advance as rapidly as the earnings of men. The obvious consequences for computing measures of occupational status result from the fact that the earnings and/or income component of an occupation which has a large concentration of women will be affected by the lower average earnings of women.

The documentation of such inequality has led to a number of attempts to explain its persistence. The explanations have focused on both the human capital or personal characteristics of women and the structural characteristics of the society and economy in which they live. The major explanations for the earnings gap focus on two interrelated factors: (1) occupational segregation by sex and the fact that women tend to be concentrated in low-paying marginal occupations and industries as a result of choice and/or discrimination, and (2) the labor force participation of women tends to be less than full time. That is, women work either part-time throughout all or part of the year or they work full time but for only part of the year to a much greater extent then men.

Concentration of Women by Occupation and Industry

Various analyses by the Bureau of Labor Statistics indicate that women are found in fewer occupations than men, and that most men are in occupations in which there are few women, and most women are in occupations that employ few men. (Fuchs, 1971, pp. 10-14). This concentration of women in relatively fewer occupations than men and occupational segregation by sex has not been entirely without benefit. One of the major areas of expansion with respect to employment opportunities has been in the service sector of the labor force. This is an area in which large proportions of women traditionally have been employed and, with the expansion of service jobs, opportunities for women have increased in, for example, the social services, health, education, welfare and personal services. There has been a concomitant decrease in domestic work, an area in which women were concentrated in the past. Based on this type of comparison with the past experience of women, there has been a significant improvement in the status of women. More of them are in service jobs and fewer in domestic jobs.

Based on a comparison with men in the same year, the picture is not as positive. In 1970, men were still overrepresented in higher level managerial jobs compared to women, who were concentrated in clerical and service occupations. Nonetheless, enough change had occurred to be measurable. Along with increasing numbers and proportions of women in the labor force, they were in a wider range of occupations in 1970 than in the past. Although still more concentrated than men, women could be found in occupations such as firefighter, policeman, trainman, etc.

It is important to note the expanded opportunities for women which existed by 1970 because the trends have continued into the eighties. It is also necessary to note that concentration in relatively fewer occupations than men was still the predominant pattern.

Dual labor market theory offers one explanation of why the concentration of women in fewer jobs contributes to the wage or earnings gap between men and women. The theory states that the labor market is divided into two major sectors, the primary and the secondary (Doeringer & Piore, 1971). The primary sector provides good jobs, wages, working conditions and opportunity for advancement, whereas the secondary sector includes poor jobs, low wages and benefits, and little opportunity for advancement. Dual labor market theory implies that in order to function efficiently the structure of the economy requires that low paying marginal jobs exist along with those in the primary sector and that these jobs will be differentially allocated to minorities and women. There is some question about the extent to which the barriers between the two sectors are impenetrable (Andrisani, 1973). The types of jobs in which women are concentrated may be found in both sectors and individual women may experience some movement between sectors.

In addition to the differential allocation of women to labor market sectors, there is differential evaluation of workers' human capital within labor market sectors. Beck and his colleagues have argued that, in both sectors, employers may allocate women to less desirable jobs, and the economic costs of such allocation are greater for women in the core than the periphery sector (Beck, *et al*, 1978). This last conclusion has been questioned (Hauser, 1979, p. 10). Canadian data also suggest that the characteristics of men and women are evaluated differently in both sectors and women are disadvantaged because they do not benefit from income-relevant characteristics such as education and work experience in the same way as men (Boyd, 1979).

It is not our purpose here to evaluate the dual labor market versus the human capital perspectives as explanations for the concentration of women in certain jobs, but merely to note that the dual labor market perspective suggests an explanation for the extensive job segregation and lower earnings of women compared to men. To the extent that women *are* concentrated in periphery sector firms or in lower echelon jobs in the core sector, their earnings will be lower than men even when performing the same jobs (Blau, 1975). Similarly qualified men and women rarely perform the same jobs, however (Sawhill 1973:385). In fact, even in traditionally "female" occupations (teaching, nursing, social work and librarianship), men dominate the better paying administrative, planning and supervisory posts (Grimm and Stern, 1974).

These empirical studies demonstrate that women are disproportionately located in low-paying jobs. The extent to which such concentration is the result of systematic bias in hiring and promotion patterns and of other factors,such as choice with respect to such things as full-time involvement in the labor force, is not entirely clear.

Full-Time Involvement in the Labor Force

As noted previously, emphasis has been given to the remarkable increase in the number of women in the labor force from 26 per cent in 1940 to 42 per cent in 1980. It is important to note also that these data are based on cross-sectional surveys measuring labor force activity at one point in time, usually one week of a given month. Sizable proportions of women are employed for only part of the year, and hence are not counted as in the labor force as measured by the survey week. For example, although 46 per cent of the women were in the labor force during the survey week in 1975, during that same year about 55 per cent of all women had been in the labor force at one time or another during the course of the entire year (U.S.D.L., 1976, p. 142). In fact, fewer than half of the women who were in the labor force worked full time the year round.

Thus the female labor force included disproportionate numbers of part-time and part-year and unemployed workers. They are what Morse (1969) called "peripheral workers." By his definition of a peripheral worker as someone who works part-time or part-year, the numerous peripherals are women. Although his work preceded some of the dual labor market theorists, he came to similar conclusions. Having documented the predominance of peripheral employment among women, he explained its persistence over time in terms of a labor force which had become bifurcated between "mainstream and marginal workers" (Morse, p. 65).

By definition, instability is a characteristic of the secondary labor market. That is, there is no job security, lay-offs are frequent and expected, etc. To the extent that women are concentrated in the secondary sector, it may contribute to the entrenched view held by many employers that women workers are highly transient. It is believed that they move in and out of the labor force because of personal characteristics associated with their family status and roles as wives and mothers. The transiency which exists may, however, be explained more by labor market characteristics, particularly their concentration in marginal jobs, than by personal characteristics.

Regardless of how it may be explained, women are disproportionately employed in occupations in which persons routinely work only part-time or part-year. Such jobs are likely to be low-status, low-paying jobs, and contribute to lowering the socioeconomic status levels of, for example, clerical and sales occupations, where women are heavily concentrated. It is felt, however, that any measure of occupational status which ignores incumbents with the lowest positions will be biased. Moreover, the historical and theoretical rationale for excluding data on women from such measures is no longer valid.

***Stratification Theory and Measures of Occupational Status*[1]**

The rationale for computing occupational status scores based solely on the characterists of men stems from a combination of historical circumstances. When the concepts of social class and socioeconomic position were first operationalized and measured in terms of occupation, there were relatively few women in the labor force, and they were concentrated in a very small number of occupations. Furthermore, when occupation was used as an indicator of socioeconomic status it was usually assumed that the family was the significant unit in the stratification system, and the occupational status of the male family head described the socioeconomic level of all family members. These and other sexist assumptions of stratification theory have been questioned in the past decade (Acker, 1973). In an era when most families were husband/wife families, and when male family heads were usually the only employed members of the family, there may have been some empirical validity for basing status measures on the characteristics of men and for assigning the scores for male family heads to all family members. Between 1950 and 1970, however, the proportion of families headed by women increased, and the stereotypical nuclear family became much less the dominant form of family in the United States. Moreover, the proportion of all women, especially of married women, in the labor force increased dramatically as noted above.

Although changes in the composition of the labor force are well documented, there have been few attempts to measure the impact of increased female labor force participation on measures of occupational status. It is only within the past few years that social scientists have seriously attempted to compare the occupational hierarchies of men and women. The evidence produced by such research indicates a high correlation between occupational status scores based solely on data for men and those based solely on data for women. After reviewing such evidence, Treiman and Terrell (1975) concluded "... there is a single occupational status hierarchy which holds for both male and female workers, and hence, that the occupational attainment of men and women legitimately can be compared by means of a single occupational scale." The single scale they suggested was based on male incumbents.

As McClendon (1976) noted, however, even though occupational status structures for men and women may be similar, that similarity

[1] This section and the next one are adapted largely from Mary G. Powers and Joan J. Holmberg, "Occupational Status Scores: Changes Introduced By the Inclusion of Women", *Demography*, Vol. 15, No. 2, May, 1978 pp. 183-204. See also Joan J. Holmberg, *Changing Occupational Status, 1960-1970: The Impact of Increased Female Labor Force Participation*, unpublished Ph.D. dissertation, Fordham University, Bronx, NY 1977.

results from quite different patterns of concentration within the occupational hierarchy. Specifically, women have been concentrated in white-collar occupational groups, particularly in clerical positions, and in blue-collar service occupations (Oppenheimer, 1970, 1973). Concentration patterns have also been noted among the male working population (Weisshoff, 1972), but men tend to be more evenly distributed throughout the occupational structure than women.

Although the current picture is still one of concentration of a large segment of the female labor force in relatively few occupations, as noted earlier, there is also evidence of a decline in job segregation accompanying the increased participation of women in the labor force (DeCesare, 1975; Garfinkel, 1975; Hedges and Bemis, 1974). It should be possible to assign women an occupational status score which is derived from a data base that recognizes their participation. Therefore, a single hierarchy of occupational status scores for the detailed occupational classification in the 1970 Census has been developed based on data for all incumbents. The classification scheme includes occupations which are predominantly segregated by sex as well as those with a more balanced mix. Insofar as the unit of analysis in this research is the occupation, and the presumption is that some objective measure of status may be attached to it, that measure is best derived from the characteristics of all incumbents - women, ethnic minorities, youth, etc.

Occupational Status Scores for Men and Women

The 1970 occupational status scores based on data for men may be compared with a set of occupational status scores derived from the characteristics of the 1970 total experienced civilian labor force, both men and women (Appendix Table A1).[*2*] Both sets of scores range from 0 to 99, with several occupations registering identical status scores. When the two sets of scores were compared, the resulting Pearson r of +.98 indicated a high correlation between the 1970 scores based on data for men and the 1970 scores based on data for the total population, both men and women, in the experienced civilian labor force. Because of the similar methodology utilized in computing both sets of scores, such a high correlation was to be expected and is consistent with the high correlation found between scores for men and women based on other data (Treiman & Terrell, 1975; Bose, 1973).

---

[2] According to the Bureau of the Census, "the experienced civilian labor force comprise: the employed and the experienced unemployed." No distinction is made between full-time and part-time workers, nor has one been made in past research using census data. Approximately 69 per cent of men and 44 per cent of women in the experienced civilian labor force worked 50-52 weeks in 1969 and 30 hours or more the week prior to the 1970 census.

Further examination of the status scores for each of the 589 detailed occupations demonstrated a tendency for the scores based on the total civilian labor force to be higher than the scores based solely on the male civilian labor force. The mean difference between the two sets of scores was +3 suggesting that the inclusion of women, who were concentrated in relatively fewer occupations and in lower status occupations, served to inflate the scores assigned higher status occupations when the total labor force was the base population (Table 5-1). In general, the analysis of the differences showed minor variations between scores based on male incumbents and scores based on

Table 5-1. Magnitude of the Difference Among 589 Occupational Status Scores Computed on the Basis of the Total Civilian Labor Force And the Male Civilian Labor Force

Point Difference	Number of Occupational Categories
0-2	193
3	44
4	56
5	39
6	44
7	44
8	36
9	30
10	32
11	30
12	15
13	11
14 or more	15
	589

all incumbents, except for 30 detailed occupations which registered significant differences.[3] The thirty occupations for which significant score differences were recorded in the two distributions did not vary in the same direction (Table 5-2). For 26 of the occupations the scores based on all incumbents were lower than scores based on male incumbents. For the other four occupations, the reverse situation occurred.

An examination of the 26 occupations which registered significant negative score-differences indicates that most of them were traditional

[3] For this study's purpose, a significant difference was defined as a difference of two standard deviations or more, 12 or more points, from the mean difference of +3. Those occupations which recorded negative differences of 9 or more or positive differences of 15 or more were classified as occupations with significant differences between the two set of scores.

Table 5-2. Occupations with Significant Differences Between Scores Calculated on the Basis of the Male Civilian Labor Force And the Total Civilian Labor Force

OCCUPATIONS:	DIFFERENCES:
Dental Hygienists	-15
Teachers, Home Economists	- 9
Teachers, except College and University (N.E.C.)*	-12
Managers and Administrators, Salaried Personal Services	- 9
Demonstrators	-33
Hucksters and Peddlers	-13
Sales Clerks, General Merchandise Stores	-12
Salesmen of Services and Construction	-10
Sales Workers-Allocated	-10
Bookkeepers	-12
Keypunch Operators	-11
Proofreaders	-16
Secretaries	-10
Stenographers	-23
Clerical Workers, Manufacturing	-10
Clerical Workers, Professional and Related Services	-18
Clerical Workers, All Other Industries	-10
Clerical and Kindred Workers-Allocated	-15
Bookbinders	-12
Operators, Ordnance	-24
Chambermaids and Maids	- 9
Child Care Workers	- 9
Hairdressers and Cosmetologists	-11
Housekeepers, except Private household	-12
School Monitors	-10
Welfare Service Orders	- 9
Home Management Advisor	+19
Teachers, Pre-kindergarten and Kindergarten	+20
Laborers-Blast Furnaces, Steel Workers Rolling and finishing Mills	+15
Laborers, Ordnance	+16

*Not elsewhere classified

female occupations, employing high proportions of women. Because women are generally paid less than men employed in the same occupation, it is not surprising that the median income level of all 26 occupations dropped substantially when women were included in the base population. In addition, for 19 of the 26 occupations, the inclusion of women resulted in a lower median educational level. For seven occupations the educational level increased or remained the same when women were included in the base population. Overall, the range of difference in the median education of men and women in these 26 occupations was not as large as the range of income differences. As a result of large differences in the median income of men and women in these 26 occupations, and the relatively large proportion of women employed in them, they received a significantly lower ranking in the occupational hierarchy based on the characteristics of all incumbents than they did in the hierarchy based on the characteristics of male incumbents.

Only four occupations recorded significant positive differences. The occupation, "Teachers, public pre-kindergarten and kindergarten," which employed a high proportion of women in 1970 showed an increased median income and a similar median education when women were included in the base. The occupation, "Home Management Advisors," which was also a female dominated occupation in 1970, recorded a decreased median income but an increased median education when women were added to the data base. The occupation, "Laborers, ordnance," which was a relatively integrated occupation in 1970, registered both an increased median income and increased median education when female incumbents were added to the base population. The male dominated occupation, "Laborers, blast furnaces, steel works, rolling and finishing mills," evidenced a decreased median income and similar median education with the inclusion of women workers in the data base.

The analysis of the 30 occupations which registered significant differences between the scores based on the characteristics of the total labor force and scores based solely on the characteristics of male incumbents points to the general effect of including women in the calculation of scores for the total list of detailed occupations. The occupational concentration of women combined with their generally lower income level served to depress the scores of 26 predominantly "female" occupations. This contributed to a general upgrading of the status position of the vast majority of the detailed occupations. Essentially, the inclusion of women in the calculation of the occupational status scores influenced the scores not only by changing the scores of those occupations which included large proportions of women, but by changing the total alignment of the occupational hierarchy. The introduction of women into the base population had a relatively large impact on a small number of occupations, and affected more modest changes in the relative status position of most detailed occupations.

Weighted Average Occupational Status Scores

Although the detailed hierarchy of occupations is regarded as the best source for the placement of individuals relative to one another, many users concerned with ranking a sample or client population by occupational status rely on the major occupational groups. Therefore, weighted average occupational scores based on data for the male labor force and on data for the total labor force were also computed for each of the major occupational groups delineated by the Bureau of the Census in 1970.[*4*] These scores are presented in Table 5-3. As expected from the strong correlation observed between the two sets of scores

Table 5-3. Weighted Average Occupational Status Scores*

Occupation	Scores Based on Male CLF	Scores Based on Total CLF
Professional, Technical and Kindred Workers	85	82
Managers & Administrators	79	80
Sales Workers	66	55
Clerical and Kindred Workers	56	51
Craftsmen and Kindred Workers	49	55
Operatives, except Transport	33	33
Transport Equipment Operators	32	42
Laborers, except Farm	15	23
Farmers and Farm Managers	20	31
Farm Laborers & Farm Foremen	4	6
Service Workers	25	24
Private Household Workers	4	4

*Based on the characteristics of the Total Experienced Civilian Labor Force (CLF) and Men in the Experienced Civilian Labor Force.

for the detailed occupational classification, a ranking of major occupational categories based on weighted average scores for the total experienced civilian labor force produced a ranking similar to that obtained from weighted scores for the male population. The category, "Professional, Technical and Kindred Workers," received the highest ranking in each population group. "Managers and Administrators" ranked second. The lowest status occupational groups also maintained similar positions whether based on data for men or for all workers. "Private

[4] The weighted average status scores were calculated by multiplying the total number employed in a particular detailed occupation by the occupation score for that occupation, then adding the figures obtained for each of the detailed occupations within a major occupational category and dividing by the total number of incumbents in the major occupational grouping.

Household Workers'' were lowest in ranking based on the total civilian labor force and equal to ''Farm Laborers and Foremen'' at the bottom of the ranking based on the male civilian labor force.

Some important differences must also be noted. Differences in the rank accorded sales workers, clerical workers and craftsmen occurred when the base shifted from male workers to all workers. In an array of weighted average scores based on data for men, sales workers ranked third, followed by clerical workers and then craftsmen. Using weighted scores based on data for the total experienced civilian labor force, sales workers and craftsmen registered identical status scores, and clerical workers ranked below these two categories. These shifts in ranking reflect the impact of including the characteristics of women in the construction of occupational status scores. Women were over-represented among sales and clerical workers in 1970 and their median income was several thousand dollars below that of men employed in sales and service occupations. The inclusion of women who were concentrated in lower level positions within each of these two broad occupational groups lowered the status positions of these occupational categories relative to craftsmen, a category in which women were significantly under-represented in 1970. This is consistent with the suggestion of some students of stratification in the United States that the differences which remain between craftsmen, sales and clerical workers, if any, are relatively small.

The different ranking assigned operatives and transport equipment operatives in each group also indicated the impact of including women in the data base. Only a small proportion of women were employed in transport equipment occupations in 1970, whereas a much larger proportion was engaged in occupations within the operative category. Given the generally lower income received by women, the presence of a large number of women in the operative category and their relative absence among transport equipment operators contributed to a much higher ranking of transport equipment operators relative to other operatives when the total experienced civilian labor force was used as the base population. Also, ''Service Workers'' dropped below ''Farmers and Farm Managers'' when women were included in the data base.

Conclusions and Implications

A comparison of occupational status scores based on data for men with scores based on data for the total experienced civilian labor force indicated important differences among specific detailed occupations as well as at the level of the major occupational groups. The scores derived from the data for all incumbents reflect occupational segregation by sex (gender) as well as the different income and educational levels of men and women in the experienced civilian labor force. They are, therefore, more valid contemporary measures of the status of occupations than scores based solely on the characteristics of men in the labor force. In short, previous findings on the socioeconomic status of occupations and of gender differences in occupational status are problematic. The social structure in which earlier measures of occupational status were developed has changed, and important theoretical and methodological issues in social stratification research require that these changes be taken into account in constructing measures of occupational status.

These findings have important implications for the use of occupation as an indicator of socioeconomic position for women and their families and for the study of the processes of status attainment. When occupation has been used to study the socioeconomic level of families in the past, the characteristics of women generally were ignored, and they were assigned the status level of male family heads. As noted previously, at an earlier time when relatively few women were in the labor force, it may have been empirically valid to assign all family members the status of the male family head. In recent years, several investigations have suggested that this practice be re-examined (DeJong *et al*, 1971; Haug, 1973; Oppenheimer, 1977). In view of the fact that women are now a significant part of the occupational hierarchy, it is important to evaluate their contribution to the socioeconomic position of their families.

If occupation is used as an index of overall socioeconomic position, and if husbands and wives tend to have the same occupational status level, it might be redundant to include a measure of occupational status for both. The extent to which the occupational status of husbands and wives are similar is an empirical question. Attempts to examine it have been hampered by the need to resort to broad occupational categories. As noted in one such study, the distinctions found between husbands' and wives' occupational levels might be due to the use of broad and heterogeneous occupational categories, and "more refined method of allocating occupations to different levels could produce a very different pattern of husband/wife job relationships" (Haug, 1973, p. 88). The occupational status hierarchy in the appendix provides such a refined method by making available a single occupational status score for detailed occupations based on data for all incumbents. The same set of scores could be used to compare husbands' and wives' occupational status. It is conceivable that families may be comprised of individuals with different levels of occupational status. The comprehensive measure of occupational status discussed here is perhaps the best general purpose indicator of occupational status for use in this area.

The increased participation of women in the labor force focused attention on status differences and income inequality by sex, and generated considerable interest in examining sex differences in the status attainment process. Until recently such studies have used the traditional measures of occupational prestige discussed earlier - all of which have been based on the labor force characteristics of men. The findings of similarity between men and women have been questioned on both methodological and theoretical grounds (Powers and Holmberg, 1978; Acker, 1973)

Several recent papers have examined the status attainment process using various measures of occupational prestige and socioeconomic status - traditional male-based scores, sex-specific scores, as well as measures based on the characteristics of the total labor force (Boyd and McRoberts, 1982; Featherman and Stevens, 1982; Cooney, Clague and Salvo, 1982). They all demonstrate that sex (gender) differences in occupational attainment vary with the particular index used. Boyd and McRoberts demonstrated that Canadian women had lower average levels of socioeconomic status than men when the measures used were based on the total labor force or were gender specific compared to male based measures. Cooney, Clague and Salvo (1982) provide a particularly broad assessment of the model used in the major studies of status attainment in the United States. Their findings, like those of Boyd and McRoberts, differ from the earlier findings of similarity between men and women. Using both the Duncan SEI and the Nam-Powers scores with data from the National Longitudinal Surveys, they demonstrated that the choice of measure influenced conclusions concerning both status levels and the process of the status attainment by gender.

Hopefully, the measure of occupational status which incorporates women into the data base will continue to inform the results of research.

REFERENCES

Acker, Joan. 1973. "Women and Social Stratification: A Case of Intellectual Sexism." *American Journal of Sociology* 78: 936-945.

Andrisani, Paul. 1973. *An Empirical Analysis of Dual Labor Market Theory.* Columbus, OH: Ohio State University Research Foundation. (Ph.D. dissertation, Ohio State University).

Beck, E.M., Patrick Horan and Charles M. Tolbert II. 1978. "Stratification in a Dual Economy." *American Sociological Review* 43: 704-720.

Blau, Francine B. 1975. *Pay Differentials and Distribution of Employment for Male and Female Office Workers.* Cambridge, MA: Harvard University Press.

Bose, Christine E. 1973. *Jobs and Gender: Sex and Occupational Prestige.* Baltimore: Johns Hopkins University, Center for Metropolitan Planning and Research.

Boyd, Monica and Elizabeth Humphreys. 1979. "Sex Differences in Canada: Incomes and Labor Markets." Paper presented at the Economic Council of Canada Conference on Incomes, Winnipeg, Manitoba.

Boyd, Monica and Hugh A. McRoberts. 1982. "Women, Men and Socioeconomic Indices: An Assessment." In Mary G. Powers, ed., *Measures of Socioeconomic Status: Current Issues.* Boulder, CO: Westview Press, pp. 129-159.

Cooney, Rosemary S., Alice S. Clague and Joseph J. Salvo. 1982. "Status Attainment of Young White Men and Women: Two Socioeconomic Measures." Mary G. Powers, *Ibid.*

DeCesare, Constance B. 1975. "Changes in the Occupational Structure of U.S. Jobs." *Monthly Labor Review* 98: 23-34.

DeJong, Peter Y., M. Brawer and S. Tobin. 1971. "Patterns of Female Intergenerational Mobility: A Comparison with Male Patterns of Intergenerational Mobility." *American Sociological Review* 36: 1033-1042.

Doeringer, Peter B. and Michael J. Piore. 1971. *Internal Labor Markets and Manpower Analysis.* Lexington, MA: D.C. Heath.

Featherman, David L. and Robert M. Hauser. 1976. "Sexual Inequalities and Socioeconomic Achievement in the U.S., 1962-1973." *American Sociological Review* 41: 462-483.

Featherman, David L. and Gillian Stevens. 1982. "A Revised Socioeconomic Index of Occupational Status: Application in Analysis of Sex Differences in attainment." In Mary G. Powers, *op. cit.*, pp. 83-127.

Fuchs, Victor R. 1971. "Differences in Hourly Earnings Between Men and Women." *Monthly Labor Review* 94: 10-14.

Garfinkel, Stuart H. 1975. "Occupations of Women and Black Workers." *Monthly Labor Review* 98: 25-35.

Grimm, James W. and Robert M. Stern. 1974. "Sex Roles and Internal Labor Market Structures: The Female Semi-Professions." *Social Problems* 21: 690-705.

Haug, Marie. 1973. "Social Class Measurement and Women's Occupational Roles." *Social Forces* 52: 86-98.

Hauser, Robert M. 1979. "On Stratification in a Dual Economy." C.D.E. Working Paper #79-46, Center for Demography and Ecology, University of Wisconsin, Madison.

Hedges, Janice M. and Stephen E. Bemis. 1974. "Sex Stereotyping: Its Decline in the Skilled Trades." *Monthly Labor Review* 97: 14-22.

McClendon, McKee J. 1976. "The Occupational Attainment Processes of Males and Females." *American Sociological Review* 41: 52-64.

Morse, Dean. 1969. *The Peripheral Worker.* New York: Columbia University Press.

Nam, Charles B., John LaRocque, Mary G. Powers and Joan J. Holmberg. 1975. "Occupational Status Scores: Stability and Changes." *Proceedings of the Social Statistics Section of the American Statistical Association,* pp. 570-575.

Oaxaca, Ronald. 1973. "Male-Female Wage Differentials in Urban Labor Markets." *International Economic Review* 14: 693-709.

Oppenheimer, Valerie K. 1970. *The Female Labor Force in the United States: Demographic and Economic Factors Governing the Growth and Changing Composition.* Berkeley: University of California Press.

Oppenheimer, Valerie K. 1973. "Demographic Influence of Female Employment and the Status of Women." *American Journal of Sociology* 78: 946-961.

Oppenheimer, Valerie K. 1977. "The Sociology of Women's Economic Role in the Family." *American Sociological Review* 42: 387-406.

Powers, Mary G. and Joan J. Holmberg. 1978. "Occupational Status Scores: Changes Introducted by the Inclusion of Women." *Demography* 15: 183-204.

Sawhill, Isabel. 1973. "The Economics of Discrimination Against Women: Some New Findings." *Journal of Human Resources* 8: 383.

Sell, Ralph R. and Michael P. Johnson. 1977-78. "Income and Occupational Differences Between Men and Women in the United States." *Sociology and Social Research* 62: 1-20.

St. Marie, Stephen M. and Robert W. Bedwerzik. 1976. "Employment and Unemployment During 1975." *Monthly Labor Review* 99: 11-20.

Sweet, James A. 1973. *Women in the Labor Force.* New York: Seminar Press.

Treiman, Donald J. and Kermit Terrell. 1975. "Women, Work and Wages: Trends in the Female Occupational Structure." In Kenneth C. Land and Seymour Spilerman, eds., *Social Indicator Models.* New York: Russell Sage Foundation.

Treiman, Donald J. and Kermit Terrell. 1975. "Sex and the Process of Status Attainment: A Comparison of Working Women and Men." *American Sociological Review* 40: 174-200.

Tyree, Andrea and Judith Treas. 1974. "The Occupational Mobility of Women." *American Sociological Review* 39: 293-302.

U.S. Bureau of the Census. *1970 Census of the Population. Subject Reports. Occupational Characteristics.* Final Report PC(2)7A. Washington, DC: U.S. Government Printing Office.

U.S. Bureau of the Census. 1973. *Current Population Reports,* Series P-60, No. 90 Washington, DC: U.S. Department of Commerce.

U.S. Bureau of the Census. 1976. *Current Population Reports,* Series P-60, No. 101, "Money Income in 1974 of Families and Persons in the United States." Washington, DC: U.S. Government Printing Office.

U.S. Department of Labor, Manpower Administration. 1976. *Employment and Training Report of the President.* Washington, DC: U.S. Government Printing Office.

U.S. Department of Labor. 1980. "Employment in Perspective: Minority Workers." *Bureau of Labor Statistics.* Report #602. Washington, DC: U.S. Government Printing Office.

U.S. Department of Labor. 1980. "Employment in Perspective: Working Women." *Bureau of Labor Statistics.* Report #600. Washington, DC: U.S. Government Printing Office.

Waite, Linda J. 1976. "Working Wives, 1940-1960." *American Sociological Review* 41: 65-80.

Weisshoff, Francine B. 1972. "Women's Place in the Labor Market." *American Economic Review* 62: 161-166.

Women's Bureau. 1976. *Women Workers Today.* Washington, DC: U.S. Department of Labor, Employment Standards Administration.

6
The Racial Factor in Occupational and Socioeconomic Status

As noted earlier, the measure of occupational status developed from census data provides scores for occupations, not persons. That is, the scores are based on the education and income properties of the occupation itself. Once a score has been assigned to each occupation and the occupations have been arranged in hierarchical order, it is possible to examine how different subgroups such as blacks and women are distributed throughout the occupational hierarchy compared to white men. A distribution of the black labor force by occupational status scores describes past and present inequalities in the allocation of occupations. Such a description of the occupational structure by race is not proof that discrimination exists, but it points to persistent patterns of selectivity which favor white over black men for high status occupations (Hodge and Hodge, 1965; Nam and Powers, 1965; Treiman and Terrell, 1975; Powers and Holmberg, 1978).

For many if not most purposes, an individual's occupation status score is a good proxy for his/her overall socioeconomic level. Yet such measures have been considered problematic for research on racial inequality because the methodology for construction of the scores is such that it heavily weighs the labor force characteristics of the white, male labor force. Whether a measure of occupational status derived from the characteristics of the predominantly white male labor force should be used to assign scores to blacks whose occupational distribution differs markedly from the white labor force has been questioned. For many purposes the general occupational status score based on all incumbents may not be the best measure of socioeconomic status for blacks.

It has been suggested that black communities assign class levels on a different basis than most objective indicators developed and standardized on the white population (Thorpe, 1972). It has been demonstrated that the same population would be differently classified as lower class and non-lower class using the Hollingshead Two-Factor Index of

Social Position, and a profile derived from research on the black situation (Thorpe, 1972). The latter identified only two significant levels - lower class and non-lower class. In a sample of southern black college students, the Hollingshead Two-Factor Index would have identified only 18 per cent as non-lower class, whereas the class profile derived from the black situation placed 61 per cent as non-lower class. Hence there may be occasions when a measure based only on blacks is preferable to one derived from the situation of the total or white population.

For most comparisons of population subgroups at national or regional levels, however, a common measure is needed. In societies such as the United States with large minority populations, several patterns of socioeconomic stratification may co-exist because each group interacts differently with the social and economic systems. Minority populations will not have the same distribution in the socioeconomic hierarchy as the dominant group for a number of reasons, not the least of which are the discriminatory practices of the dominant group which limit access to high status positions.

In the United States blacks have faced serious long-term restrictions in their attempts to achieve higher educational and occupational levels and, hence, higher income (Spear, 1967). A comparison of black and white populations in the early part of the twentieth century indicated a rather well developed white class structure with several clearly defined classes and a black class structure consisting of a large urban and rural lower class and a small middle class in occupations requiring little education and/or formal training - entertainment and the clergy (Spear, 1967; Landry, 1979). Various white ethnic groups also experienced concentration at the lower end of the scale.

Between 1960 and 1970, various ethnic and racial groups still differed significantly with respect to social and economic characteristics including their education, occupation and income. Although such differences among white ethnic groups appear to have narrowed in recent decades, there is still considerable occupational selectivity and segregation of the black population when compared to whites. A number of evaluations of socioeconomic trends in the United States have noted the persistence of differentials by race, along with significant improvement for select categories of blacks, notably the young and women (Farley and Hermalin, 1972; Glenn, 1974; Hauser and Featherman, 1974; U.S. Bureau of the Census, 1975; Featherman and Hauser, 1976). Thus, although ethnic inequality and stratification is still a basic feature of American society, inequality among white ethnic groups appears to be diminishing. Among blacks, however, inequality in the labor force was still apparent in 1970, both in terms of high unemployment and differential occupational distribution. It has been cogently argued that the high unemployment levels and low status jobs of blacks may be explained, in part, by the historical circumstance of their entry into the urban industrial labor force at a significant point in the conflict between unions and the capitalist mode of production, and their role in that conflict (Bonacich, 1976). The persistence of such inequality through the 1970's demands further examination and explanation.

This chapter presents data on inequality among black and white persons in the United States in 1960 and 1970 as measured by the Census multiple-item SES and occupational scores. Because this was a period of rapid social change and of civil rights and affirmative action programs aimed at improving the status of blacks, it is of pragmatic as well as theoretical importance to examine trends in inequality by race.

The Socioeconomic Status of Blacks in 1960

Previous analysis of data derived from tabulations of the national 1/100 sample enumerated in the 1960 Census of Population compared the socioeconomic standing of the white and nonwhite (largely black) populations (Nam, Powers and Glick, 1964). Nonwhites were over-represented among the population with low socioeconomic scores and under-represented among the population with high status scores. Nonwhites comprised 11 per cent of the total population in 1960, but 42 per cent of the total population in the lowest tenth of socioeconomic scores and less than two per cent of those in the highest tenth of socioeconomic scores (Table 6-1).

Table 6-1. Per cent Distribution of the Population, by Color within Socioeconomic Status Categories, United States: 1960

Socioeconomic status score	Total	White	Nonwhite
Total population	100.0	88.8	11.2
90 to 99 (high)	100.0	98.5	1.5
80 to 89	100.0	97.9	2.1
70 to 79	100.0	96.5	3.5
60 to 69	100.0	96.2	3.8
50 to 59	100.0	94.4	5.6
40 to 49	100.0	89.8	10.2
30 to 39	100.0	84.1	15.9
20 to 29	100.0	78.5	21.5
10 to 19	100.0	72.4	27.6
0 to 9 (low)	100.0	58.4	41.6

Source: Charles B. Nam, Mary G. Powers and Paul C. Glick, "Socioeconomic Characteristics of the Population: 1960," U.S. Bureau of the Census, *Current Population Reports,* Series P. 23, No. 12, 1964, p. 2.

Alternatively, 35 per cent of the nonwhites and nine per cent of the whites had socioeconomic scores below 20, whereas two per cent of the nonwhites and 15 per cent of the whites had scores of 80 or above (Table 6-2). These differences in socioeconomic scores by color persisted in different types or residence areas, although nonwhites showed the same general pattern by residence as the total population. That is, more persons with high status scores were found in the urban fringes of medium to large size cities than anywhere else, and rural farm areas contained proportionately the most persons with lowest status scores and the fewest persons with the highest scores (Table 6-3) (Nam, Powers and Glick, 1964).

Table 6-2. Socioeconomic Status of the Population, by Color, United States: 1960

Socioeconomic status score	Total	White	Nonwhite
Total population	100.0	100.0	100.0
90 to 99 (high)	5.4	5.9	0.7
80 to 89	7.8	8.6	1.5
70 to 79	11.2	12.2	3.5
60 to 69	13.6	14.8	4.6
50 to 59	15.1	16.1	7.6
40 to 49	14.0	14.1	12.8
30 to 39	11.6	11.0	16.5
20 to 29	9.3	8.3	18.0
10 to 19	7.6	6.2	18.8
0 to 9 (low)	4.3	2.8	15.9

Source: Charles B. Nam, Mary G. Powers and Paul C. Glick, "Socioeconomic Characteristics of the Population: 1960," U.S. Bureau of the Census, *Current Population Reports,* Series P. 23, No. 12, 1964, p. 2.

Further analysis of the 1960 data focused on a comparison of white and nonwhite family heads (Nam and Powers, 1965). Because there were well-known differences in socioeconomic status by type of residence as well as by race and ethnic categories, the SES distribution of family heads was made by both race and residence (See Figure 4-1 in Chapter 4). As noted in that earlier comparison:

> Since the distribution for all family heads combined is essentially normal, with a slight skewness toward the lower levels, group differences in socioeconomic status can be viewed graphically in terms of departures from a normal distribution. (Nam and Powers, 1965).

In 1960, clearly a much larger proportion of nonwhite family heads than of white family heads were concentrated in the lower half of the range of scores. Both white and non-white family heads exhibited a

Table 6-3. Socioeconomic Status of the Population, by Color and Type of Residence, United States: 1960

Socioeconomic status score and color	United States	Urbanized areas: Central Cities	Urbanized areas: Urban Fringe	Other Urban	Rural Nonfarm	Rural Farm
Total......... thousands...	179,580	57,856	37,833	29,860	40,473	13,558
Per cent..........	100.0	100.0	100.0	100.0	100.0	100.0
80 to 99............	13.2	13.7	22.8	12.2	7.7	2.8
50 to 79..........	40.0	42.4	50.1	40.1	34.4	18.1
20 to 49................	34.9	35.2	23.4	36.0	40.6	46.3
0 to 19	11.9	8.6	3.7	11.7	17.3	32.9
White...... thousands...	159,513	47,703	36,126	27,062	36,709	11,913
Per cent.........	100.0	100.0	100.0	100.0	100.0	100.0
80 to 99..............	14.6	16.0	23.7	13.3	8.5	3.1
50 to 79................	43.0	46.8	51.3	43.2	37.4	20.3
20 to 49	33.4	31.1	22.0	35.1	40.8	49.8
0 to 19..............	9.0	6.1	3.0	8.5	13.4	26.9
Nonwhite..... thousands...	20,067	10,153	1,707	2,798	3,764	1,645
Per cent.........	100.0	100.0	100.0	100.0	100.0	100.0
80 to 99.................	2.2	3.0	3.6	1.9	0.7	0.4
50 to 79................	15.8	21.9	25.2	10.5	4.8	2.1
20 to 49.............	47.3	54.5	52.7	44.3	38.8	21.2
0 to 19.................	34.7	20.6	18.4	43.3	55.7	76.3

Source: Charles B. Nam, Mary G. Powers and Paul C. Glick, "Socioeconomic Characteristics of the Population: 1960," **U.S. Bureau of the Census, *Current Population Reports*, Series P. 23, No. 12, 1964**, p. 2.

more favorable socioeconomic distribution in central cities and the urban fringes of these cities than in the rural areas and small towns and cities outside urbanized areas. Among nonwhite family heads, concentration in the lowest third of the SES range was especially marked outside urbanized areas. These areas also had a small nonwhite elite in the highest SES level, which probably consisted of professional and business people serving the nonwhite community, especially in segregated communities. Although small, it was proportionately larger than the highest SES group in urbanized areas.

There has been a long tradition of research on the residence patterns of race and ethnic groups - especially of their movement out of areas of original settlement in city neighborhoods and into lower density suburban areas. The latter is frequently viewed as indicative of cultural assimilation and upward mobility. Such urban research generally defines the metropolitan community as the Standard Metropolitan Statistical Area (SMSA) and compares city and suburban components of the population. In addition to the comparison of white and nonwhite family heads noted above, the socioeconomic levels of the total, nonwhite and selected white ethnic populations in 1960 were examined in various residence categories including metropolitan areas (Powers, 1968). Those data were derived from tabulations of the national five per cent sample of the 1960 Census and the Census socioeconomic status scores were again used. This large and statistically highly reliable sample provided a socioeconomic distribution of the population by color and nativity for the U.S. as a whole and for various residence categories (Table 6-4).

A more favorable socioeconomic distribution of both white and nonwhite persons was found in SMSAs than outside SMSAs. The foreign-stock population was more like native-white persons of native-parentage than like the black, Puerto Rican or Spanish surname populations. In each residential area the native whites of native or foreign parentage had the highest median status scores and blacks had the lowest.

All of the ethnic populations were highly urban in 1960, and were concentrated in SMSAs. Hence, it was important to examine the SES distribution of the various population subgroups in different types of metropolitan communities. Size of metropolitan area appeared most important in view of other research (Schnore, 1964). In all parts of the SMSAs in 1960 the black population occupied the lowest rung of the socioeconomic ladder (Table 6-5).

The foreign-born population of southern European origin (the then recent immigration groups) had the lowest median scores among the white population, but their median scores were considerably higher than those for blacks in each residence category. All subgroups fared best in the largest SMSAs, and the highest median scores for all

Table 6-4. Median SES Score of the Population, by Color and Nativity, and of Selected "Minority" Populations, by Residence, United States: 1960

Color and Nativity	United States	In SMSA'S			Not in SMSA'S		
		Central Cities	Urban Ring	Rural Ring	Urban	Rural non-Farm	Rural Farm
Total population	51.7	53.6	62.7	50.7	51.5	41.1	28.6
White native, native parentage	54.7	58.4	64.6	52.5	54.7	44.3	32.1
White, foreign or mixed parentage	56.6	57.7	62.9	52.9	51.8	45.0	27.3
White, foreign born	28.4	35.0	35.8	22.6	23.2	16.5	10.3
Selected Minority Populations							
White, Spanish surname	32.2	36.0	43.6	21.5	25.1	19.8	12.5
Puerto Rican stock	34.3	33.6	43.8	41.2	34.9	43.7	18.5
Negro	27.5	34.9	33.5	21.1	4	15.7	9.9

Source: Mary G. Powers, "Class, Ethnicity and Residence in Metropolitan America," *Demography* 5:1 (1968): 443-448.

Table 6-5. Median SES Scores of Selected Nativity and Ethnic Groups, and of the Negro Population in SMSA'S by Size of SMSA: 1960

Residence in the SMSA, by size of SMSA	White Native Parent-age	Native-European Parentage: Area of Europe: North and West	Central and East	South	Foreign born-European: Area of Europe: North and West	Central and East	South	Negro
In all SMSA'S	60.1	60.3	62.8	56.1	52.6	46.7	42.2	33.9
Central cities	58.4	58.3	61.9	54.3	59.7	46.9	50.7	34.9
Urban part of ring	64.6	64.1	65.5	58.7	56.7	50.6	44.8	33.5
Rural part of ring	52.5	53.4	53.3	54.0	48.0	35.3	38.8	21.1
In SMSA'S of 1,000,000 and over	62.7	61.9	64.3	56.8	53.8	47.9	43.1	37.7
Central cities	58.6	59.0	62.8	54.6	51.4	46.5	41.7	38.0
Urban part of ring	66.7	65.5	67.4	59.7	58.3	52.8	46.0	37.9
Rural part of ring	56.4	56.4	55.0	55.0	50.9	37.5	41.0	26.8
In SMSA'S of 250,000 to 1,00,000	58.1	57.7	59.1	54.9	49.9	42.8	40.4	29.7
Central cities	58.1	57.3	59.5	53.8	48.8	43.4	39.5	30.8
Urban part of ring	61.7	60.3	60.5	56.6	52.4	44.6	41.8	27.8
Rural part of ring	51.3	52.5	52.9	54.1	46.8	33.5	39.7	22.3
In SMSA'S of less than 250,000	56.4	55.7	57.2	53.1	48.9	41.6	38.6	26.0
Central cities	58.5	56.9	59.1	53.2	49.2	43.2	38.5	28.3
Urban part of ring	58.3	58.2	56.8	53.8	51.4	40.6	41.2	25.3
Rural part of ring	50.3	49.3	50.7	51.0	44.3	35.7	32.8	17.9

Source: Mary G. Powers, "Class, Ethnicity and Residence in Metropolitan America," *Demography* 5:1 (1968): 443-448.

groups were found in the urban part of the ring of SMSAs (the suburbs). The position of blacks relative to all others remained the same in all residence categories - they had the lowest median scores.

Although they were at the bottom of the socioeconomic status ladder in all parts of the metropolitan area, blacks fared better in metropolitan areas than in nonmetropolitan areas. They also fared better in areas where there were relatively large white foreign-stock populations than in areas of low foreign-stock concentration (Powers, 1978).

Not only were blacks concentrated in the lower end of the range of scores in 1960, but more black family members participated in the labor force at all levels (Powers and Wendell, 1972). At that time a larger proportion of black families than of white families had two or more persons in the labor force (48 per cent compared to 38 per cent). Multiple labor force participation of family members was associated with higher SES of family heads in both white and black families (Table 6-6). Among black families with two or more persons in the labor force, the largest proportion of family heads was in the third quartile of the range of scores, whereas the largest proportion of such white families was in the second quartile of the range. Multiple wage-earners in white families contributed toward "comfortable" or above the middle level status whereas, in black families, multiple wage earners contributed to almost attaining middle level status.

In short, in 1960 the socioeconomic status of blacks and black families, as measured by the multiple-item SES score, was much lower than that of most of the white population. The relationship held in various residence areas among both family heads and individuals. The relatively low position of blacks was thoroughly documented using the multiple-item score. (See Chapter 7 for later changes in socioeconomic patterns by race.)

The Occupational Status of Blacks in 1970

By 1970, the occupational status score by itself, rather than the multiple-item score, came to be used as an index of socioeconomic status for blacks as well as for the total population.

The 1970 census figures indicate that blacks were over-represented in lower status occupations such as service workers, operatives, laborers, and private household workers, and under-represented in high status occupations such as professional, technical and kindred workers, and craftsmen. For example, about 16 per cent of all white persons in the labor force were in technical, professional and kindred occupations compared to only about eight per cent of all blacks who were in the labor force (Table 6-7). In contrast, less than one per cent of the white labor force was classified as private household workers compared to about eight per cent of the black labor force.

As noted in an earlier chapter, factors such as age, race and sex might have been incorporated into the construction of the occupational status score itself because of the differential distribution of occupations along racial, sex and age lines. Even though occupational status varies among these subcategories of the population, these items were not built into the score itself because the object was to develop a national standard of occupational status in order to observe whatever patterns of occupational variation might be found among various subpopulations. Had subcategories such as age, race and sex been incorporated as components of the score, it would not have been possible to observe variations among these subgroups.

Table 6-6. Socioeconomic status of Family Heads in Husband-Wife Families by Race and Number of Persons in the Labor Force, United States: 1960

Race and Number in the Labor Force	Total		SOCIOECONOMIC STATUS SCORES			
	Number	Per cent	99-75	74-50	49-25	24-0
All Families	39,657,243	100.0	20.3	36.5	30.0	13.4
None in the LF*	3,055,983	100.0	4.3	13.5	32.7	49.5
1 in the LF	21,341,846	100.0	21.0	35.6	31.3	12.2
2 in the LF	12,400,578	100.0	22.9	41.8	27.4	7.9
3+ in the LF	2,858,836	100.0	21.5	45.2	26.0	7.3
White Families	36,464,491	100.0	21.6	38.2	29.1	11.2
None in the LF	2,821,814	100.0	4.6	14.3	34.0	47.1
1 in the LF	19,907,573	100.0	22.3	37.1	30.6	10.1
2 in the LF	11,214,638	100.0	24.4	43.9	26.2	5.5
3+ in the LF	2,520,466	100.0	23.3	47.8	24.1	4.8
Negro Families	2,933,639	100.0	4.4	16.1	39.2	40.3
None in the LF	215,169	100.0	.2	2.9	16.7	80.2
1 in the LF	1,313,609	100.0	2.1	13.4	41.3	43.2
2 in the LF	1,095,487	100.0	7.4	19.7	40.5	32.4
3+ in the LF	309,374	100.0	6.7	24.3	40.9	28.1

*LF=Labor Force

Source: Powers and Wendell, 1972. (See References)

Table 6-7. Occupational Distribution of the Experienced Civilian Labor Force by Race: 1970

Occupation	White Labor Force	Black Labor Force
Total	71,789,302	7,854,433
Per cent	100.00	100.00
Professional, Technical & Kindred Workers	16.10	7.80
Managers and Administrators, except Farm	8.68	2.21
Sales Workers	7.53	2.29
Clerical and Kindred Workers	18.08	13.58
Craftsmen and Kindred Workers	14.31	9.03
Operatives, except Transport	13.46	18.48
Transport Equipment Operatives	3.67	5.55
Laborers, except Farm	4.10	9.59
Farmers and Farm Managers	1.91	.55
Farm Laborers and Farm Foremen	1.12	2.46
Service Workers, except Private Household	10.21	19.94
Private Household Workers	.76	8.16
Unemployed Persons	.09	.15

Source: U.S. Bureau of the Census, *Census of Population: 1970, Detailed Characteristics,* Table 224, pp. 746-748.

Standards for Status of Blacks: Black vs. Total Population

At the same time, it is necessary to recognize, as noted earlier, that many socioeconomic indices, because they are standardized for whites, may not adequately describe the socioeconomic makeup of blacks, particularly within small local communities. Research focusing on local communities might rely on more subjective evaluations and measures of prestige rather than objective measures based on the total population. There are also potential uses for alternative sets of scores calculated for different subgroups. Relatively few blacks have gained access to managerial and other high status positions. As a result of this, the criteria for evaluating occupations may differ somewhat in black communities than in the white population. There may be some utility in having an occupational status score which reflects only the characteristics of black incumbents available for research focusing strictly on a black community. In the following analysis, scores generated separately for the black population but not presented in this volume are compared with scores for the white population.

Special tabulations of data from the 1970 census were required to tabulate occupational status scores separately based on data for white men and women and black men and women in the experienced civilian labor force. The original list of 589 occupations was reduced to 335 in order to make viable comparisons among men and women. In some occupations there were very few women, particularly black women. In each of these cases the occupation was combined with another occupation. No incumbents in the sample were lost; the occupational categories were recombined and occupational status scores for all incumbents in 335 occupations were calculated.* In order to examine the effect of race on occupational status, occupational status scores were constructed separately for the white experienced civilian labor force and the black experienced civilian labor force. In keeping with the earlier argument that the total scores for both sexes provide the best indicator of occupational status, the following analysis compares scores for each race category which include both men and women.

Occupational status scores based on data for the black civilian labor force were considerably higher than occupational scores based on data for the white civilian labor force because of the concentration of blacks at the bottom of the occupational hierarchy. The differences between the two sets of scores ranged from minus 44 to plus 49 with a mean difference of about 15 points.

Only two occupations, both in manufacturing industries, showed no differences between the scores when calculated on the basis of data for the black civilian labor force and the white civilian labor force. These were sales representatives and operatives in manufacturing industries. The scores were 88 for the former and 21 for the latter whether calculated on the basis of data for blacks or whites. Twenty-six occupations exhibited lower occupational status scores when calculated on the basis of data for the black civilian labor force than when calculated on data for the white incumbents. These 26 ranged throughout the whole array of occupations from professionals such as architects and teachers at the top to various categories of farm laborers, foremen, etc. at the bottom. The remaining 307 occupations showed scores which were generally higher when calculated on the basis of data for the black civilian labor force than for the white. The differences ranged from a low of 2 or 3 points to a high of 49 point difference. Table 6-8 shows the number of occupations in each of several categories of difference between the two sets of scores.

As noted earlier, the mean difference in the occupational status scores as calculated on the basis of data for the black and white civilian labor force separately was 15 with a standard deviation from the mean of 12.5. Of the 335 occupations, 148 showed differences of 0 to 15 points, another 164 showed differences of 16 to 30 points, and 23 showed differences of 30 points or more. The 23 occupations showing

---

*We wish to thank Ruth Gindin for the tabulations and computer work required to recombine the detailed occupations and for calculating the occupationsl status scores for 335 occupations.

Table 6-8. Differences between Occupational Status Scores Based on the Black Labor Force and Those Based on the White Labor Force, United States: 1970

Point Difference	Number of Occupations
0-5	48
6-10	43
11-15	57
16-20	52
21-25	69
26-30	43
31-35	15
36-40	3
41-45	3
46-50	2

Source: Unpublished tabulations by authors.

differences of 30 points or more were primarily skilled and semi-skilled occupations, i.e., tailors, textile operatives, painters, etc., and included no professional, technical and managerial occupations. Nor did they include many sales or clerical personnel (Table 6-9). Apparently the greatest differences in status scores occur among the blue collar occupations, particularly those having some degree of skill. The continued clustering of the black labor force in jobs at the bottom of the occupational hierarchy has been thoroughly documented (Garfinkel, 1975). This clustering at the bottom of the hierarchy tends to raise scores for most occupations when the occupational status scores are calculated solely on data for the black labor force.

The reason for this may be found in the historical patterns of differentiation in the education and income levels of the black and white populations in the United States. Even when in the same occupation, black incumbents tend to have lower income levels than white incumbents. For example, the special tabulation of the 1970 census data used in this research showed that the median income of black architects was only $8,000 compared to $13,529 for white architects. In addition, the median educational level of black architects was 12.9 years compared to 17.5 years among white architects. In the comparison of occupational scores based on data for the black and white civilian labor force separately, architects were one of the few occupations which had a lower score based on data for black incumbents. However, the difference was only 3 points: 99 for whites and 96 for blacks. In most cases, the median income for white incumbents was higher than that for blacks, although there were some exceptions, notably, librarians, bank tellers and musicians. The differences with respect to the median educational level of an occupation also generally favored the white

Table 6-9. Occupations Exhibiting Differences of 30 Points or More in Scores Based on the White Civilian Labor Force and Scores Based on the Black Civilian Labor Force

Occupation	Difference
Foresters and Conservationists	—44
Payroll and Timekeeping Clerks	31
Engravers, except Photoengravers	38
Shoe Repairmen	46
Tailors	36
Blasters and Powdermen	43
Metalworking Operatives, except Precision Machine	33
Milliners	38
Painters, Manufactured Articles	31
Sewers and Stitchers	35
Shoemaking Machine Operatives	33
Textile Operatives	35
Fabricated Metal Industries, Including Not Specified MET	31
Manufacturing Operatives—Durable Goods:	
Miscellaneous Manufacturing Industries	32
Apparel and Other Fabricated Textile Products	31
Not Specified Manufacturing Industries	32
Operatives, except Transport-Allocated	32
Bus Drivers	49
Parking Attendants	33
Lumbermen, Raftsmen and Woodchoppers	—32
Farm Managers	—43
Baggage Porters and Bellhops	34
Guards and Watchmen	35

Source: Unpublished tabulations by authors.

incumbents but the differences were not as large as the income differences. Although it is not possible to evaluate the relationship between education and income by race from these data, they certainly suggest that the economic return to education is lower for blacks than it is for the white civilian labor force. This is consistent with other research (Stolzenberg, 1975; Siegel, 1965). Obviously some of the differences in the median level of education and median income of the occupations are explained by differences in the age and sex composition of black and white incumbents. These would be significant control variables in studies seeking to explain such differences. Insofar as each incumbent is weighted individually in deriving an occupational status score, however, the overall score is the result of a simple average of the characteristics of all of the incumbents included in the composition.

Because the occupational status scores are calculated as cumulative percentage distributions based on the number of persons in each detailed occupation and all of those *below*, the scores are higher when based solely on black incumbents because of the large concentration of blacks in occupations at the bottom of the occupational hierarchy. This concentration serves to raise the status of occupations in the middle and of those closer to the top. A larger proportion of the black civilian labor force than of the white is located below the middle level occupations. Thus, assigning an occupational score based on all persons or all white persons to the black population might serve to lower the relative status of many middle and upper level blacks if comparisons are to be made strictly among blacks. Where comparisons with the total population or other parts of it are desirable, scores based on the characteristics of all incumbents are probably the best ones to use (Lencyk, 1978)

REFERENCES

Bonacich, Edna. 1976. "Advanced Capitalism and Black/White Relations in the United States: A Split Labor Market Interpretation." *American Sociological Review* 41: 34-51.

Farley, Reynolds and Albert Hermalin. 1972. "The 1960s: A Decade of Progress for Blacks?" *Demography* 9: 353-370.

Featherman, David L. and Robert M. Hauser. 1976. "Changes in the Socioeconomic Stratification of the Races, 1962-73." *American Journal of Sociology* 82: 621-651.

Garfinkel, S.S. 1975. "Occupations of Women and Black Workers." *Monthly Labor Review* 98: 25-35.

Glenn, Norval D. 1974. "recent Changes in the Social and Economic Conditions of Black Americans." In Joseph Lopreato and Lionel S. Lewis, ed., *Social Stratification: A Reader.* New York: Harper and Row, pp. 447-455.

Hauser, Robert M. and David L. Featherman. 1974. "White-Nonwhite Differentials in Occupational Mobility Among Men in the United States, 1967-72." *Demography* 11: 247-265.

Hodge, Robert W. and Patricia Hodge. 1965. "Occupational Assimilation as a Competition Process." *American Journal of Sociology* 71: 249-264.

Landry, Bart. 1979. "Mobility Patterns and Class Formation Among Blacks and Whites in the United States." Paper presented at the annual meeting of the American Sociological Association, Boston.

Lencyk, Ann. 1978. *The Influence of the Black Labor Force Participation on Occupational Status Scores.* Unpublished M.A. thesis, Fordham University.

Nam, Charles B. and Mary G. Powers. 1965. "Variations in Socioeconomic Structure by Race, Residence and the Life Cycle." *American Sociological Review* 30: 97-103.

Nam, Charles B., Mary G. Powers and Paul C. Glick. 1964. "Socioeconomic Characteristics of the Population: 1960." *Current Population Reports,* Series P-23, No. 12. Washington, DC: U.S. Government Printing Office.

Powers, Mary G. 1968. "Class, Ethnicity and Residence in Metropolitan America." *Demography* 5: 443-448.

Powers, Mary G. 1978. "Ethnic Concentration and Socioeconomic Status in Metropolitan Areas." *Ethnicity* 5: 266-273.

Powers, Mary G. and Frana S. Wendell. 1972. "Labor Force Participation and Socioeconomic Status." *Sociological Quarterly* 13: 540-546.

Powers, Mary G. and Joan J. Holmberg. 1978. "Occupational Status Scores: Changes

Introduced by the Inclusion of Women." *Demography* 15: 183-204.

Schnore, Leo F. 1964. "Urban Structure and Suburban Selectivity." *Demography* 1: 164-176.

Siegel, Paul. 1965. "On the Costs of Being Negro." *Sociological Inquiry* 35: 41-57.

Spear, Allen H. 1967. *Black Chicago: The Making of a Negro Ghetto, 1890-1920.* Chicago: University of Chicago Press.

Stolzenberg, Ross M. 1975. "Education, Occupation and Wage Differences Between White and Black Men." *American Journal of Sociology* 81: 299-323.

Thorpe, Claiburne B. 1972. "Black Social Structure and White Indices of Measurement." *Pacific Sociological Review* 15: 495-506.

Treiman, Donald J. and Kermit Terrell. 1975. "Sex and the Process of Status Attainment: A Comparison of Working Women and Men." *American Sociological Review* 40: 174-200.

U.S. Bureau of the Census. 1975. "The Social and Economic Status of the Black Population in the United States, 1974." *Current Population Reports,* Special Studies, Series P-23, No. 54. Washington, DC: U.S. Government Printing Office.

U.S. Bureau of the Census. *Census of Population: 1970 Detailed Characteristics.* Washington, DC: U.S. Government Printing Office.

7
Stability and Change in Occupational and Socioeconomic Status

The components of status have obviously been changing over time. Educational levels have risen as greater and greater proportions of the population gained access to more schooling. Income levels have gone up with spiralling inflation and growth in national productivity. And the occupational structure has been upgraded with rapidly increasing numbers of professional, technical, managerial, and other white-collar jobs and only slightly-rising or declining numbers of blue-collar and farm-related positions.

As a result of these changes, what was once regarded as an adequate educational level may be deemed inadequate in today's world. What was once a livable income will probably be regarded as below an acceptable level. Even an occupation that one's father was engaged in may not command the same status for the son.

What we are saying is that the whole status structure of American society has been altered with time, thereby modifying the chances that any individual will end up in a particular *absolute* status level. But have *relative* status levels changed very much? Everyone's status may improve in an absolute sense and still the same kinds of disparities may remain, placing some persons as much above or below other persons as they would have been before.

The question of relative status changes can be addressed pointedly with regard to occupations and composite measures of socioeconomic status. How stable are indicators of occupational status over time? To the extent that change has taken place, what has been the nature of that change? Can we identify critical factors related to changes? Have socioeconomic inequalities among groups increased, decreased, or remained the same?

Changes in Occupational Prestige

Students of social stratification have written about the apparent stability of occupational prestige, or the perceived rankings of occupations, from both spatial and temporal points of view.

Hodge, Siegel, and Rossi (1964) reported that: "Despite rather extensive searches conducted by a variety of techniques, it appears that occupational prestige hierarchies are similar from country to country and from subgroup to subgroup within a country." Treiman (1977) drew on studies of sixty different societies around the world to reach the conclusion that the prestige structures of occupations were indeed stable. Based on comparisons of occupations which were common across cultures, he found an overall correlation coefficient of .79 in prestige ratings. The correlations varied among pairs of countries but, with few exceptions, they were of a high order.

If estimates of prestige tend to be fairly common from society to society, does that mean that they also do not change over time within the same society? Hodge, Siegel, and Rossi (1964) compared occupational prestige ratings in the United States based on samples of Americans interviewed in NORC surveys in 1947 and in 1963, and even extended the comparisons back to 1925 with reference to earlier samples studied by Count. On the basis of occupations which could be matched, an overall correlation coefficient of .93 was calculated for the 1925-1963 comparison. The comparison of 1947 and 1963, which encompasses a shorter time span and a larger number of occupations rated on a more comparable basis, resulted in a correlation of .99. Although some occupations were accorded higher prestige and some were assigned lower prestige in the later studies, the authors concluded that "there have been no substantial changes in occupational prestige in the United States since 1925."

Changes in the Socioeconomic Aspect of Occupational Status

We have argued before that prestige and socioeconomic dimensions of occupation are critically different. It is therefore of interest to assess the stability of occupational status on the latter as well as the former ground. This was first done by comparing 1950 and 1960 estimates of the socioeconomic ratings of the full range of detailed occupations (Nam and Powers, 1968).

There were two main objectives to the study: (1) to measure the extent of stability of occupational statuses between 1950 and 1960 using socioeconomic status criteria, and (2) to classify those occupations with significantly changing statuses according to several variables that might help to explain the changes. Correlation analysis was used to measure the degree of stability between the two sets of scores. Specific occupations which had quite different scores at the two dates are examined in terms of changes over the decade in the number employed in the occupation, the median age of occupants, the median educational level of persons in the occupations, and their median income level. The first two variables provide clues to the recruitment and reduction processes of the occupation; the latter two variables are components of the changing status level of the occupations.

Product-moment correlation coefficients were computed for the total list of detailed occupations and for occupations within the major subgroups. The overall correlation coefficient is .96, indicating a very close association between the 1950 and 1960 scores (Table 7-1). This high correlation is consistent with our notion of general stability in the status hierarchy of occupations, particularly over a period of time as short as ten years.

Table 7-1. Product-moment Correlation Coefficients of Scores Assigned Detailed Occupations on the Basis of 1950 and 1960 Data, by Major Occupation Groups

Major Occupation Group	Number of Occupations	Correlation Coefficient (r)
*All nonfarm occupations**	460	.96
Professional, technical and kindred workers	58	.94
Managers, officials, and proprietors	58	.95
Clerical and sales workers	40	.88
Craftsmen, foremen, and kindred workers	75	.95
Service workers (incl. private household)	35	.85
Operatives and kindred workers	123	.89
Laborers	71	.81

Regression equation of 1950 on 1960 scores:

$$Y = a + bX$$

$$Y = 11.25 + .9036X$$

*Six farm occupations, plus those in the Armed Forces or with occupations not reported were not included; the correlation remains about the same whether or not they are included.

Coefficients of correlation for the major occupation groups were not as high, however. They ranged from .95 for managers, officials, and proprietors, and for draftsmen, foremen, and kindred workers, to .81 for laborers. Hodge, Seigel, and Rossi, in their study of occupational prestige changes between 1947 and 1963, found consistently high correlations, of the order of .96 to .99, among occupational groupings, including groups of manual and of farm occupations. Part of the inconsistency between their findings and ours may be explained by the small, and perhaps selective, sample of occupations in their study, but the inconsistency might also reflect the greater stability of prestige than of socioeconomic ratings of occupations. That is, for some occupations prestige ratings may persist even when the relative socioeconomic position of the occupation is changing. Some support for this interpretation is found in the correlation coefficient of .83 between prestige scores from the NORC study for 1963 and socioeconomic scores of occupations based on the 1960 Census for a matched list of occupations. This correlation, and the still smaller correlations for major groupings, is lower than between either types of score at successive dates. It suggests that, for many occupations, a prestige criterion may not be the best way to validate socioeconomic scores of occupation.

Out of 466 detailed occupational categories, only 23 had identical socioeconomic scores in 1950 and 1960 (Table 7-2). The scores for 45 of the occupations rose over the decade while the scores for 398 declined. Since the same procedure was used to calculate the scores at the two dates and the two sets of scores are, in effect, normalized, it may seem peculiar that such a high proportion of occupations had declining scores between 1950 and 1960. The explanation appears to lie in the fact that during the decade, a great number of occupations toward the lower end of the status scale either declined in numbers or increased in numbers but not at the rate of higher status occupations, thereby depressing the scores at many points in the distribution. Another way of stating this effect is that persons in a given occupation which maintained its relative status rank between 1950 and 1960 had relatively fewer persons below them on the status scale in 1960 than in 1950; as a result, their status scores was lower. This phenomenon of declining status was characteristic of some occupations in all major groupings, but was less pronounced among white-collar occupations, especially professional and technical workers.

In those cases where differences in occupational scores existed, we were interested in knowing what factors were associated with the differences. Calculations were made of the relationship between score changes during the decade and the four variables examined (the number employed in the occupation, the median age of occupants, the median educational level of occupants, and their median income). During the decade, slightly less than half of all occupations declined in the number of occupants while slightly more than half increased in numbers. This particular fact is interesting in view of the increasing size of the labor force between 1950 and 1960. It reflects the principal expansion of the labor force in white-collar and skilled occupations as indicated by the much higher proportion of occupations in the white collar and craft fields with increasing numbers of occupants.

Median age is significant to our analysis because an occupation with an increasing median age is usually one which is declining in numbers and either is not recruiting many younger persons, or is recruiting mainly older persons to join those already in the occupation who have been aging over the decade, or is selectively losing younger persons from the field, or some combination of these. While two-thirds of all

Table 7-2. Changes in the Status Scores of Detailed Occupations, by Major Occupation Group, 1950 to 1960

Major Occupation Group	Grand Total	Decrease (points)				No Change	Increase (points)			
		Total	11+	6-10	1-5		1-5	6-10	11+	Total
Number										
Total	466*	398	103	145	150	23	29	9	7	45
Prof., tech., and kdrd. wkrs.	58	39	3	7	29	10	7	1	1	9
Mgrs., officials & propr's., exc. farm	58	53	5	18	30	1	3	1	—	4
Clerical and kdrd. wkrs.	28	26	8	14	4	1	1	—	—	1
Sales workers	12	10	1	2	7	—	1	—	1	2
Craftsmen, foremen, & kdrd. wkrs.	75	66	14	25	27	2	6	—	1	7
Operatives and kdrd. wkrs.	123	111	46	46	19	5	3	4	—	7
Private household wkrs.	6	5	3	1	1	—	—	—	1	1
Other service wkrs.	29	24	7	6	11	—	2	2	1	5
Laborers, exc. farm and mine	71	59	14	25	20	4	6	—	2	8
Farmers and farm mgrs.	2	2	—	1	1	—	—	—	—	—
Farm laborers and foremen	4	3	2	—	1	—	—	1	—	1
Per cent										
Total	100	85	22	31	32	5	6	2	2	10
Prof., tech., and kdrd. wkrs.	100	67	5	12	50	17	12	2	2	16
Mgrs., officials, and propr's., exc. farm	100	91	9	31	52	2	5	2	—	7
Clerical and kdrd. wkrs.	100	93	29	50	14	4	4	—	—	4
Sales workers	100	83	8	17	58	—	8	—	8	17
Craftsmen, foremen, and kdrd. wkrs.	100	88	19	33	36	3	8	—	1	9
Operatives and kdrd. wkrs.	100	90	37	37	15	4	2	3	—	6
Private household wkrs.	100	83	50	17	17	—	—	—	17	17
Other service wkrs.	100	83	24	21	38	—	7	7	3	17
Laborers, exc. farm and mine	100	83	20	35	28	6	8	—	3	11
Farmers and farm mgrs.	100	100	—	50	50	—	—	—	—	—
Farm laborers and foremen	100	75	50	—	25	—	—	25	—	25

*Excludes a small number of occupations which could not be matched in 1950 and 1960.

occupations have employees with increasing median age, a rising median age was found to be less typical of occupations in the professional and technical, and clerical and sales fields, than of those in other fields.

An increasing median educational level between 1950 and 1960 was characteristic of a vast majority of occupations. It may also be noted that rising education was found among a high proportion of occupations in all major groupings. In one sense, this should not be too surprising since it reflects the democratization of education in the United States. On the other hand, this suggests that educational differences in the society were persisting, though at a somewhat higher level, and that a tendency toward equalization of education among occupations has probably not yet occurred.

Even more universal than the rising educational level of occupations was their rising income level. Only one per cent of the detailed occupations had a decreasing median income level, and this pattern was common to all major groupings. A rise in absolute incomes in the 1950's was shared by nearly everyone. The fact remained, however, that the greatest increases in median income were found among white-collar occupations, particularly some professional, technical, and managerial occupations. The general rise in income for occupations, however, did not alter the relative position of most individual occupations with respect to income. This is suggested by the very high correlation of .96 between 1950 and 1960 median income figures for all occupations. Similar high correlation coefficients were found within each major occupational subgroup.

Out of the 466 detailed occupations, 49 were dropped from the more detailed analysis of occupations because of noncomparable classification in 1950 and 1960. Of the 417 occupational categories which had comparable occupational titles at the two dates, only 18 had identical status scores at each date. The scores for 39 of the 417 occupations rose over the decade while the scores for 360 declined. Because of the shifting score pattern between 1950 and 1960, it did not seem advisable to interpret any change in scores, or even relatively small changes in scores, as being meaningfully different. Since our main objective in examining discrepancies in scores of specific occupations was to see what characteristics of occupations were associated with significant changes in scores, we decided to analyze further those occupations for which the ratings differed by more than ten points at the two census dates. The particular cutoff, while arbitrary, was selected on the basis of an inspection of the distribution of score changes; there seemed to be a natural break in the distribution at about this cutoff point.

There were 92 occupations with scores differing by more than ten points at the two dates. Only four of these had increasing scores and 88 had dereasing scores. In an effort to discover common factors associated with their changing statuses, these occupations were classified simultaneously by the direction of change in their status score, number of occupants, median age, median educational level relative to the average for all occupations, and median income level relative to the average for all occupations. The data are rather striking, since they show the principal concentration of these occupations into four groupings. All four include occupations with declining status and increases in educational and income levels below the national average. Two groups were increasing in size, one of these groups having an increasing median age and the other a decreasing median age. Two of the groups were decreasing in size, likewise one with declining average age and the other with a rising average age.

The five discrepant occupations outside these four groupings include the four with rising status and one with declining status. ''Pattern and model makers'' have rising status due to sharp increases in both education and income, and this is associated with increasing numbers in the occupation and decreasing median age. This occupation seems to be drawing its recruits from young, well-educated men. ''Laborers in photo equipment manufacturing'' also have rising status because of both disproportionately higher education and income and the median age of the occupants is declining, but it is an occupation which is declining in size. ''Hucksters and peddlers'' have higher status in 1960 than 1950 solely because of their sharp educational increase. Their numbers are increasing and they are getting younger but the return in income to the occupation did not increase at the national rate. ''Professional athletes,'' the fourth of the group with sharply-rising status scores, derived their higher status from a large increase in median income while their numbers declined somewhat and their median age increased. This perhaps reflects the cutbacks and failures of minor leagues in the professional sports as much as it does the improved salary-bargaining positions of the athletes.

Of the four groupings of sharply-declining status occupations, all of which had increases in education and income below the national average, those with an increasing number of occupants and an increasing median age would seem to be recruiting mainly older men who are shifting from other jobs which are declining in numbers. Typical occupations in this group are ''bus drivers,'' ''self-employed proprietors of retail eating and drinking trade,'' ''messengers and office boys,'' ''operatives in business and repair services,'' ''housekeepers and stewards,'' and ''farm foremen.''

The group declining sharply in status with an increasing number of occupants but with decreasing median age would seem to be recruiting younger men and/or losing older men. Typical of such occupations are ''cashiers,'' ''bank tellers,'' ''recreation and group workers,'' ''guards, watchmen, and doorkeepers,'' and ''gardeners.''

The third group of occupations with substantially lower status scores in 1960 than in 1950 is that with decreasing numbers of occupants and increasing medium age. These occupations seem to be largely those which are declining in importance or which are giving way to automation or to other mechanized processes. Among these occupations are "tailors," "bakers," "loom fixers," "upholsterers," "operatives" and "laborers" in many industries, and "book-binders."

The final group of occupations among those with sharp declines in status include those decreasing in both numbers and median age. Being diminishing occupations, these are either recruiting younger men of generally low status (e.g., "apprentices" in various trades) or are losing older men through retirement or death (e.g., "railroad inspectors," "dyers," and some "operatives").

An examination of the racial composition of these occupations in 1950 and 1960 showed little change in the per cent black between the two dates; for most of the occupations, the change was hardly discernible.

Our study of changes in the status level of workers by occupation between 1950 and 1960 reveals several facts about the occupational structure in the United States of interest to students of social stratification.

1. In conformity with earlier studies, we find a high degree of overall stability in the status patterns of occupations. There is some indication, however, that the observed degree of stability based on socoieconomic criteria is not quite as high as that based on a prestige criterion, at least for some segments of the occupational structure.

2. The relative status levels of an exceedingly high percentage of occupations were lower in 1960 than in 1950, owing to a general depression of the status structure brought about by decreasing relative numbers of persons in lower status occupations and corresponding increasing relative numbers in higher status occupations. As a result of this general depression of status scores, an occupation which maintained its relative rank among occupations between 1950 and 1960 found more persons at the later date in occupations with higher status and fewer persons in occupations with lower status.

3. An examination of four characteristics of occupations showed that for all detailed occupations as a group: (a) despite an increasing size of the labor force, roughly half of the occupations declined in numbers between 1950 and 1960; (b) about two-thirds of the occupations had a rising median age; (c) an increasing median educational level was characteristic of a vast majority of occupations; and (d) virtually all occupations increased in median income level, although at different rates.

4. Among occupations with sharply changing status scores (nearly all of which had declining statuses), increases in both median educa-

tion and median income were below the national average. These occupations could be differentiated, however, by their varying combined patterns of changing numbers in the occupation and changing median age, which reflect types of recruitment to the occupation and loss of occupants through retirement, transfer, or death.

The American social stratification system, as indexed by socioeconomic scores of occupation, thus seems to have been altered in an interesting fashion in the 1950-60 decade. During this period of general affluence in our society, the education and income levels of most occupations rose. At the same time, however, the occupational distribution shifted, placing more persons at the upper end of the hierarchy. Relatively more persons in the higher status occupations served to depress the status scores for many occupations by (a) making many higher status occupations more common and, hence, having relatively fewer persons in occupations below them, and (b) making the lower status occupations less common but, likewise, resulting in relatively fewer persons in those occupations and occupations below them on the scale.

The same type of analysis was performed for the decade from 1960 to 1970 by Nam, LaRocque, Powers, and Holmberg (1975). It is a troublesome task to measure changes in the status level of occupations over time since the occupational classification system of the Bureau of the Census is modified at each census period. In calculating and comparing status scores for 1950 and 1960, Nam and Powers developed a common list of detailed occupations for the two dates by combining occupations that were subdivided or merged. Only a relatively small percentage of occupations did not have identical titles at the two dates.

In 1970, however, a major reclassification of the occupational list was made. New occupational titles were identified in order to (1) increase the homogeneity of the detailed occupations and (2) to reduce the number of persons listed under occupations n.e.c. (not elsewhere classified). In addition, some job titles were shifted from one major group to another because of the changing nature of the work; some categories were eliminated and the components combined with other occupations; and some occupations that had large numbers of incumbents were subdivided where occupational distinctions could be made within them. As a result, anyone who tries to compare detailed occupations for 1960 and 1970 is faced with an almost insuperable undertaking.

It was only possible to establish essential matches for 126 detailed occupations. Most of these were classified identically in the 1960 and 1970 censuses, but some were changed slightly so that no more than one per cent of the incumbents were classified differently in the two censuses. Although we cannot claim that the 126 occupations are a representative selection of the total 589 occupations in the detailed list, the matched occupations cover all major groupings and the distribution of status scores is not unlike that of the complete list.

When Nam and Powers compared the full list of detailed occupations for men for 1950 and 1960, they calculated a correlation coefficient between the two sets of scores of .96. The 1950-1960 correlation coefficient using the 126 occupations is .95. The calculation for men in the 126 occupations in 1960 and 1970 provides a correlation coefficient of .97, indicating that an extremely high degree of stability in status scores has been maintained. Even the correlation coefficient between scores for men in 1950 and 1970 is .91. For all women combined, the coefficient for 1960-1970 was .85, reasonably high but much lower than for men. Apparently, the changing roles of women in recent years has modified the status levels of some occupations in a significant way.

An examination of the scores for specific occupations shows that, while for the vast majority of occupations the status scores changed very little between censuses, for a minority of occupations the changes were notable and most often in a downward direction.

Additional analysis of 1960-1970 changes in occupational status scores was undertaken by Terrie (1979). He treated 128 matched occupations as though they constituted the total occupational structure and recalculated occupational status scores based on that group alone. The data bases used were the 1960 and 1970 one-per cent public-use sample records of the census. An analytical model was developed which treated median earnings and median education as the immediate (or endogenous) determinants of an occupation's status and median age, per cent female, per cent nonwhite, per cent unemployed, per cent employed part-time, per cent working year-round, and per cent newcomers to the occupation as indirect (or exogenous) determinants.

Regression analysis showed that per cent unemployed and per cent employed part-time accounted for an insignificant amount of variance in both earnings and education. Earnings and education contributed about equally to determination of overall status, although the importance of education was relatively greater in 1970 than 1960. The age factor operated mainly through education and the sex factor primarily through earnings. The race dimension, proportion working year-round, and per cent of newcomers exerted some effects on both earnings and education.

The 1960-1970 analysis also revealed a continuation of the phenomenon observed for 1950-1960 whereby the status scores of more occupations fell than rose. Moreover, 40 of the 128 occupations shifted at least five ranks in the status array over the decade. Twenty of them changed 10 or more places. As many as 39 occupations had status scores in 1970 which were six points or more different from that in 1960.

The picture which emerges is one which identifies the total occupational status structure as being fairly stable over time but which likewise points to a considerable amount of intrastructural dynamics with the fortunes of particular occupations rising and falling each decade. This research also indicates that, up until now, changing occupational status scores are more likely to have been the result of modifications in relative education than relative earnings positions of the occupations.

The Future of Occupational Status

For two decades, in the post-World War II period, the occupational structure in the United States underwent considerable change, the main features of which were increasing participation and continual upgrading through a rapidly expanding white-collar labor force. At the same time, the socioeconomic status pattern of occupations was not altered in the same manner. Disparities among occupations in regard to status remained wide and most occupational groups retained their relative location in the status hierarchy. Yet, the status positions of a number of occupations did change significantly owing to the inability of some occupations to keep pace in educational and income advancement.

What changes in occupational status do take place reflect evolving social processes in American society. Population developments resulting in geographical redistribution of people and a shifting age profile lead to differences in the supply of workers in various occupations and to the characteristics of occupational incumbents. Better access of women and minority group members to jobs from which they had been largely excluded earlier adds to the supply side as well. Modernization, technological growth, and consequent alterations in the economy change occupational demands, both numerically and in terms of the types of workers who are most desirable to fill the places.

Ultimately, the average status levels of occupations depend on their relative education and income positions. It is difficult to project these reliably into the future. We do know from the past, however, that measured educational differences among all groups in the country have been narrowing and increasing homogenization can be expected. Income differences, on the other hand, have not narrowed correspondingly and some group differences have continued to widen. Some have argued that the economic dimension of status will always persist and, based upon it, social strata in our nation will continue to be notably differentiated. It is also argued by some that apparent reductions in educational inequalities are illusory because more equal numbers of school years completed are masking critical disparities in educational quality.

When occupational scores for 1980 are calculated, we will be able to answer some of the questions that arise in the area of stability and change in occupational status. The considerable modification in the census occupational classification system in 1980 will limit our opportunity to do so, but it will be possible to execute some kinds of relevant analysis.

Changes in the Overall Socioeconomic Structure

In Chapter 4 we discussed some properties of the multiple-item socioeconomic measures as revealed by analysis of the 1960 Census of Population five percent sample. Variations by race, residence, and stage of the life cycle (indicated by age of the family head) were observed in both the distribution of socioeconomic status and the pattern of status consistency.

We have since used the 1976 Survey of Income and Education conducted by the Census Bureau to replicate those measures and analyses. As a result, comparisons of socioeconomic structure in the American population for the period 1960 to 1976 can be made. In order to maximize the comparisons, we have limited the analysis to certain categories of variables that can be measured the same way at both dates.

Table 7-3 includes 1960 and 1976 distributions of family heads in the United States by socioeconomic status, differentiated by race, metropolitan status, and age of the head. Several generalizations can be made about the time comparisons: (1) The overall SES distribution remains relatively unchanged except for some slight shifts in the middle socioeconomic range and a minor decline at the lowest socioeconomic levels. Not much change would have been expected because of the relatively short time period (16 years). (2) The disparity between white and black family heads remained pronounced, but a significant drop in the lowest SES category was observed for blacks with some compensating shift into the middle SES categories. (3)The SES distribution for residents of metropolitan areas shifted downward while that for family heads in nonmetropolitan areas moved upward, thereby measurably reducing the differential between the two that had existed in 1960. (4) Age patterns of SES were similar at the two dates, despite some apparent downgrading of the distribution for the youngest family heads. (5) Overall, socioeconomic differentiation was as observable among these categories in 1976 as in 1960, although the narrowing of metropolitan-nonmetropolitan differences and the sharp decline of low-status blacks were meaningful changes.

In Table 7-4, socioeconomic levels of family heads are cross-tabulated with status consistency types, separately for whites and blacks in 1960 and 1976. Allowing for the variability which arises from

Table 7-3. Distribution of Family Heads by Socioeconomic Score, by Selected Characteristics, United States: 1960 and 1976

	1960						
Characteristics	Total	80 to 99 (high)	60 to 79	40 to 59	20 to 39	0 to 19 (low)	Median score
All family heads	100.0	13.8	25.8	29.0	20.7	10.7	53.1
White	100.0	14.8	27.6	29.8	19.3	8.5	55.2
Black	100.0	2.6	8.0	20.3	35.1	34.0	28.5
Metropolitan	100.0	17.0	29.4	29.9	17.6	6.2	57.8
Nonmetropolitan	100.0	8.2	19.5	27.4	27.1	18.8	43.7
14-24 years old	100.0	3.9	25.0	39.4	25.6	6.2	49.5
25-44 years old	100.0	16.6	30.5	29.7	17.3	5.9	58.2
45-64 years old	100.0	14.2	24.3	29.5	21.4	10.7	52.3
65 years and over	100.0	7.0	15.0	21.1	28.0	28.8	35.0

	1976						
Characteristics	Total	80 to 99 (high)	60 to 79	40 to 59	20 to 39	0 to 19 (low)	Median score
All family heads	100.0	13.7	24.3	31.7	21.7	8.6	54.4
White	100.0	14.7	25.8	32.2	20.1	7.3	54.1
Black	100.0	4.1	11.6	28.3	36.0	20.0	36.7
Metropolitan	100.0	13.9	24.8	31.8	21.1	8.4	52.9
Nonmetropolitan	100.0	12.5	22.3	31.0	24.6	9.5	52.2
14-24 years old	100.0	1.9	14.9	42.2	32.9	8.1	44.3
25-44 years old	100.0	16.8	28.1	33.4	17.6	3.9	57.0
45-64 years old	100.0	14.8	25.7	31.7	21.3	6.5	54.0
65 years and over	100.0	7.1	14.3	21.5	29.5	27.6	35.2

Sources: U.S. Bureau of the Census, *1960 Census of Population, PC[2]-5C, Socioeconomic Status,* Table 7; and unpublished tabulations from the 1976 Survey of Income and Education.

sampling errors at the two dates, the status configurations are exceedingly similar at the two time periods. One notable change is the rising proportion of inconsistent cases where education and occupation are consistent but income is high. This may be a reflection of larger government transfer payments which add to income without changing educational and occupational statuses, as well as an increase in the number of wives and other family members contributing to family income.

One conclusion from the analysis of these tables is that relatively stability in socioeconomic status characterizes American society but that some change has been occurring. A second conclusion is that multiple-item measures may reveal more about socioeconomic structure than occupation alone by taking account of more dimensions of, and greater variance in, socioeconomic status.

A Theoretical Postscript on Socioeconomic Measurement

This book has focused on a socioeconomic measurement approach to social stratification. It offers several techniques for converting the

Table 7-4. Status Consistency Type by Socioeconomic Status Level, for Family Heads, by Race, United States: 1960 and 1976

Race and status consistency type	1960					
	All SES levels	80 to 99 (high)	60 to 79	40 to 59	20 to 39	0 to 19 (low)
WHITE						
Total	100.0	100.0	100.0	100.0	100.0	100.0
All components consistent	28.9	63.1	26.5	8.6	17.3	73.7
2 components consistent	61.6	36.9	64.2	73.7	73.7	26.3
Income high	10.8	2.9	12.0	14.8	12.2	2.8
Income low	13.6	10.3	16.6	16.2	11.6	4.4
Education high	5.3	1.1	3.7	4.2	4.1	3.1
Education low	15.8	15.0	18.0	20.1	12.9	1.8
Occupation high	11.0	1.0	6.5	10.0	25.3	13.9
Occupation low	5.3	6.7	7.4	5.9	2.4	0.3
All components inconsistent	9.6	—	9.3	17.7	9.0	—
Occup. high, income low	1.4	—	1.1	2.6	1.9	—
Occup. high, educ. low	1.4	—	0.7	2.8	2.1	—
Educ. high, occup. low	0.4	—	0.3	0.8	0.3	—
Educ. high, income low	1.3	—	1.1	2.1	2.1	—
Income high, occup. low	1.0	—	2.1	1.3	0.2	—
Income high, educ. low	4.0	—	4.0	8.1	2.5	—
BLACK						
Total	100.0	100.0	100.0	100.0	100.0	100.0
All components consistent	35.3	63.6	21.9	9.5	14.5	73.0
2 components consistent	57.0	36.4	67.9	71.4	76.8	27.0
Income high	8.9	2.3	11.3	15.7	11.1	2.4
Income low	12.5	19.7	26.9	17.4	16.4	1.6
Education high	10.2	2.1	6.0	13.8	14.3	5.4
Education low	8.7	3.4	8.0	10.8	14.0	2.6
Occupation high	13.0	0.2	2.7	6.1	18.6	14.8
Occupation low	3.7	8.6	13.0	7.6	2.5	0.1
All components inconsistent	7.7	—	10.2	19.1	8.6	—
Occup. high, income low	0.9	—	0.9	2.5	0.9	—
Occup. high, educ. low	0.8	—	0.2	1.4	1.5	—
Educ. high, occup. low	0.4	—	1.1	1.1	0.2	—
Educ. high, income low	2.3	—	2.0	4.5	3.4	—
Income high, occup. low	0.6	—	3.6	1.6	0.1	—
Income high, educ. low	2.7	—	2.5	8.0	2.6	—

Table 7-4 (Continued):

Race and status consistency type	All SES levels	80 to 99 (high)	60 to 79	40 to 59	20 to 39	0 to 19 (low)
	1976					
WHITE						
Total	100.0	100.0	100.0	100.0	100.0	100.0
All components consistent	32.2	70.7	20.6	24.0	20.0	66.9
2 components consistent	60.6	29.3	73.3	62.2	74.1	33.1
Income high	20.2	4.1	17.1	24.7	28.3	22.2
Income low	8.3	8.7	12.2	5.8	9.1	1.9
Education high	4.6	2.6	5.2	4.3	7.2	1.3
Education low	14.7	4.3	26.7	11.8	15.3	2.8
Occupation high	5.1	0.7	4.7	7.1	6.1	4.0
Occupation low	7.7	8.9	7.4	8.5	8.1	0.9
All components inconsistent	7.2	—	6.0	14.0	5.8	—
Occup. high, income low	0.3	—	0.2	0.8	0.2	—
Occup. high, educ. low	0.8	—	0.5	1.4	1.0	—
Educ. high, occup. low	0.4	—	0.2	0.8	0.6	—
Educ. high, income low	0.5	—	0.8	0.7	0.5	—
Income high, occup. low	1.8	—	0.9	4.6	0.2	—
Income high, educ. low	3.4	—	3.4	5.7	3.3	—
BLACK						
Total	100.0	100.0	100.0	100.0	100.0	100.0
All components consistent	34.2	69.6	22.9	25.6	25.1	63.0
2 components consistent	58.9	30.4	69.5	60.9	69.2	36.9
Income high	20.1	2.8	16.9	22.3	20.7	21.4
Income low	9.4	4.7	13.9	9.6	12.5	1.8
Education high	7.7	4.4	6.4	5.8	11.6	4.6
Education low	8.5	3.2	16.7	7.6	10.1	3.1
Occupation high	4.4	1.5	3.9	5.6	4.6	3.4
Occupation low	8.8	13.8	11.7	10.0	9.7	2.6
All components inconsistent	6.9	—	7.6	13.5	5.7	—
Occup. high, income low	0.3	—	0.1	0.7	0.1	—
Occup. high, educ. low	0.4	—	0.5	0.8	0.4	—
Educ. high, occup. low	0.4	—	0.4	0.8	0.3	—
Educ. high, income low	0.8	—	1.3	1.4	0.7	—
Income high, occup. low	2.0	—	2.6	5.1	0.6	—
Income high, educ. low	3.0	—	2.7	4.7	3.6	—

socioeconomic characteristics of persons into indicators of one's position in the societal hierarchy, and it illustrates the use of these indicators to describe and analyze certain patterns of social inequality in American society.

Being essentially methodological and empirical in substance, it may strike readers that the volume is atheoretical and lacking in conceptual relevance. We would like to counter that point of view by stating briefly and cogently our perception of the theoretical rationale for the proposed measurement and some theoretical consequences of our empirical analysis. In part, these comments recapitulate what might be discovered at various points throughout the book. However, some theoretical significance may have been left implicit instead of being stated explicitly.

Our measurement approach accepts, in principle, the Weberian notion of "class, status, and party" as three essential components of social stratification. Each of these adds another dimension to understanding the complexity of the stratifying process. The class component is concerned with socioeconomic criteria, the basis for an individual's life chances. The status component reflects the prestige, honor, and esteem assigned by others to one's positions in the system. The party component, according to Weber, dealt with the exercise of power over others and the influence and authority one derives from attachment to certain membership and interest groups.

Most work by social scientists on the measurement of social stratification has been related to the first two of those dimensions. It has been argued elsewhere (Nam and Terrie, 1981), and is a major thesis of our presentation here, that many measures in social stratification confuse the "class" and "status" components. The two are sometimes used interchangeably, and indicators of one are frequently used to gauge the rankings of persons on the other.

We have tried to make a clear distinction between status (prestige) and class (socioeconomic) criteria and have focused our attention on the latter. Of course, to some degree the two are correlated, but they also possess some unique characteristics. Evaluations of where people stand in the social hierarchy sometimes lag behind changes (upward or downward) in more objective indications of ranking. On occasions, the objective indications change with time as a result of more subjective perceptions of social standing.

The three measures that we have developed and used for the past two decades are all designed to tap the socioeconomic-class component of stratification. The *occupational status score* is based on purely socioeconomic indicators. It is crude or imperfect to the extent that occupational categories each embrace an array of specific job types which may not be homogeneous as to socioeconomic elements. Yet, occupation is a convenient identifier of individuals that is more readily observable than other identifiers which indicate socioeconomic condition. Hence, it is often a sole source of socioeconomic measurement. The *multiple-item SES score* was constructed to compensate for some of the deficiencies of the occupation-alone measure. Combining the occupational status score with education and family or household income indicators serves to specify some of the variance within occupations when they are scored simply. Therefore, the multiple-item score is a refinement of the occupational status score. It does require more information from data sources and is more extensive for calculation purposes. These factors limit its use, even though it is conceptually and methodologically preferable. The *status consistency type* complements the other two measures by describing the pattern of the multiple items making up the second score. Within SES categories, the contributions of the several variables may differ from individual to individual or family to family. These patterns may reflect a stage of life-cycle development and also show the origins of one's socioeconomic status placement.

It should be clear that the way in which persons are placed in the stratification system by any of these measures has a bearing only on their "class" position, and that positions on status (prestige) and party (power) dimensions are not so indicated. For many research and decision-making purposes, our measures are exactly what is intended. That is, if it is the objective living conditions or prospect for life-chances one wants to identify, our socioeconomic approach is preferable to other approaches. If prestige or power dimensions of stratification are desired, other measures would be preferred.

To the extent that we continue to clarify the purposes of using specific measures of social stratification as well as the underlying assumptions of the measures used, we will come closer to making our analyses more relevant and our contributions to theoretical formulations more germane.

REFERENCES

Hodge, Robert W., Paul M. Siegel and Peter H. Rossi. 1964. "Occupational Prestige in the United States: 1925-1963." *American Journal of Sociology* 70: 286-302.

Nam, Charles B., John LaRocque, Mary G. Powers and Joan J. Holmberg. 1975. "Occupational Status Scores: Stability and Change." *Proceedings of the American Statistical Association, Social Statistics Section,* pp. 570-575.

Nam, Charles B. and Mary G. Powers. 1968. "Changes in the Relative Status Level of Workers in the United States, 1950-1960." *Social Forces* 47: 158-170.

Nam, Charles B. and E. Walter Terrie. 1981. "Measurement of Socioeconomic Status from United States Census Data." In Mary G. Powers, ed., *Measures of Socioeconomic Status: Current Issues.* Boulder, CO: Westview Press.

Terrie, E. Walter. 1979. *Factors Associated with Occupational Status Changes in the U.S., 1960 to 1970.* Unpublishedd. dissertation, Florida State University.

Treiman, Donald J. 1977. *Occupational Prestige in Comparative Perspective.* New York: Academic Press.

Appendixes:

GUIDE
To Occupational and Socioeconomic Status Scores

Three socioeconomic measures have been described in this work. In Chapter 3, the procedures for calculating *Occupational Status Scores* were presented. This measure is to be used when one wants to use only *occupation* as an indicator of socioeconomic level.

In Chapter 4, the procedures for deriving a *multiple-item measure of socioeconomic status* [*SES*] and a *status consistency type* were described. These latter measures can be calculated when one has data for individuals on *occupation, education,* and *household income,* and when more refined indicators of socioeconomic status are preferred.

The appendixes to follow provide requisite data in the form of a *Scoring Guide* for quickly and easily deriving the above measures. There are certain steps that will facilitate their calculation. Let us assume that you have a data source which includes for each individual an entry on occupation, the number of years of school completed, and the amount of household income.

For ***Occupational Status Scores:***

It is advisable to (1) search in the U.S. Bureau of the Census, *Alphabetical Index of Industries and Occupations,* 1971, for the occupational entry for the individual;

(2) Note the numerical 3-digit or alphabetic code for the detailed occupational category in which the particular occupational description falls;

(3) Determine the verbal description of the detailed occupational category by searching for that number or letter in the classification given in the front of the Census report,

(4) Find that detailed occupational category in Table A1 in the

appendix of this book, and

(5) Note the occupational status score given for that occupational category.

For ***Multiple-Item SES*** and ***Consistency*** Measures:

Perform the following steps:

(1) Use the occupational status score for the individual as given above.

(2) Find the educational category in which the individual falls in Table B1 in the appendix, and record the score.

(3) Find the appropriate income category in Table B2 in the appendix and record that score.

(4) Sum these three scores and average them by dividing the sum by three. This gives the multiple-item SES score.

(5) Using the information provided in Chapter 4 about the assignment of status consistency-inconsistency types, compare the three scores and identify the resulting status consistency type.

The convenient **SCORING GUIDE** for these measures now follows.

TABLE A1

Occupational Status Scores for 589 Occupations*
For Total Labor Force, Men, Women, and Working Women, Full-Time, 1970

Occupation	Status Score: Total	Men	Women	Women Working Full-time
Professional, Technical and Kindred Workers				
Accountants	89	88	87	87
Architects	97	95	99	100
Computer Specialists				
Computer Programmers	89	84	95	97
Computer Systems Analysts	93	91	96	97
Computer Specialists (N.E.C.)**	93	91	94	95
Engineers				
Aeronautical and Astronautical	96	96	96	98
Chemical	97	96	98	97
Civil	95	93	96	98
Electrical and Electronic	95	94	96	97
Industrial	93	91	93	94
Mechanical	95	94	96	98
Metallurgical and Materials	96	95	96	97
Mining	94	92	96	97
Petroleum	96	95	96	97
Sales	94	93	96	97
Engineers (N.E.C.)**	94	93	96	98
Farm Management Advisors	94	90	87	97
Foresters and Conservationists	78	70	37	49
Home Management Advisors	77	58	94	98
Lawyers and Judges				
Judges	99	98	95	100
Lawyers	99	98	100	100
Librarians, Archivists and Curators				
Librarians	75	72	94	98
Archivists and Curators	80	72	91	97
Mathematical Specialists				
Actuaries	94	97	92	92
Mathematicians	96	97	97	98
Statisticians	88	91	94	95
Life and Physical Scientists				
Agricultural	91	87	68	93
Atmospheric and Space	95	95	82	98
Biological	91	91	96	98
Chemists	94	92	97	98
Geologists	97	97	87	98
Marine	96	95	96	98
Physicists and Astronomers	99	98	99	99

Life and Physical Scientists (N.E.C.)	97	97	96	98
Operations and Systems Researchers and Analysts	91	88	95	94
Personnel and Labor Relations Workers	89	89	90	92
Physicians, Dentists and Related Practitioners				
Chiropractors	95	93	70	97
Dentists	99	98	91	99
Optometrists	99	98	98	96
Pharmacists	94	93	91	97
Physicians, Medical and Osteopathic	99	99	100	100
Podiatrists	99	98	80	100
Veterinarians	99	98	93	100
Health Practitioners (N.E.C.)	94	87	99	100
Registered Nurses, Dietitians and Therapists				
Dietitians	56	51	77	83
Registered Nurses	66	62	87	91
Therapists	73	72	88	92
Health Technologists and Technicians				
Clinical Laboratory Technologists and Technicians	70	68	88	90
Dental Hygienists	70	85	91	95
Health Record Technologists and Technicians	68	55	90	89
Radiologic Technologists and Technicians	64	70	79	85
Therapy Assistants	54	61	59	39
Health Technologists and Technicians (N.E.C.)	63	64	75	61
Religious Workers				
Clergymen	77	68	62	59
Religious Workers (N.E.C.)	59	61	59	70
Social Scientists				
Economists	96	95	95	97
Political Scientists	98	97	99	99
Psychologists	96	96	100	100
Sociologists	94	93	95	99
Urban and Regional Planners	95	91	96	99
Social Scientists (N.E.C.)	91	91	89	99
Social and Recreation Workers				
Social Workers	82	80	93	96
Recreation Workers	58	57	56	90
Teachers, College and University				
Agriculture	97	95	95	99
Atmospheric and Space	96	94	64	99
Biology	96	95	95	100
Chemistry	97	95	96	100
Physics	97	94	100	99
Engineering	98	97	88	99
Mathematics	95	92	95	99
Health Specialties	96	98	99	100
Psychology	96	97	100	100
Business and Commerce	95	95	96	98
Economics	98	97	100	99
History	95	93	98	100
Sociology	94	93	96	100
Social Science Teachers (N.E.C.)	96	95	100	100
Art, Drama and Music	92	91	90	99

Coaches and Physical Eduction	94	91	99	99
Education	98	98	100	100
English	91	91	96	99
Foreign Language	89	91	95	99
Home Economics	87	96	99	100
Law	99	98	95	99
Theology	91	88	94	99
Trade, Industrial and Technical	90	89	86	99
Miscellaneous Teachers, College and University	94	92	99	100
Teachers, College and University, Subject Not Specified	87	89	83	99
Teachers, Except College and University				
Adult Education	81	84	81	91
Elementary School				
Public	80	79	95	96
Private	66	67	79	88
Pre-kindergarten and Kindergarten				
Public	72	52	92	91
Private	47	55	52	53
Secondary School				
Public	86	85	98	98
Private	77	75	89	91
Teachers, Except College and University (N.E.C.)	52	64	55	91
Engineering and Science Technicians				
Agriculture and Biological Technicians, Exc. Health	65	60	70	70
Chemical Technicians	79	72	86	82
Draftsmen	80	73	87	86
Electrical and Electronic Engineering	82	76	77	73
Industrial Engineering	79	74	84	82
Mechanical Engineering	86	80	72	82
Mathematical	86	81	85	82
Surveyors	72	61	38	79
Engineering and Science Technicians (N.E.C.)	77	67	83	77
Technicians, Except Health Engineering and Science				
Airplane Pilots	94	93	95	76
Air Traffic Controllers	85	84	88	82
Embalmers	75	65	83	76
Flight Engineers	91	89	83	76
Radio Operators	60	57	50	49
Tool Programmers, numerical control	87	83	91	76
Technicians (N.E.C.)	79	67	88	83
Vocational and Educational Counselors	92	91	99	99
Writers, Artists and Entertainers				
Actors	71	64	85	92
Athletes and Kindred Workers	56	54	47	68
Authors	90	89	92	97
Dancers	40	47	40	50
Designers	89	87	88	95
Editors and Reporters	86	89	91	95
Musicians and Composers	49	45	49	83
Painters and Sculptors	77	81	71	89
Photographers	75	69	57	56
Public Relations Men and Publicity Writers	91	90	91	96

Radio and Television Announcers	71	59	59	89
Writers, Artists and Entertainers (N.E.C.)	80	80	76	94
Research Workers, Not Specified	86	88	87	97
Professional, Technical and Kindred Workers (N.E.C.)	72	76	78	89
Managers and Administrators, Except Farm				
Assessors, Controllers and Treasurers, Local Public Administration	67	71	65	61
Bank Officers and Financial Managers	90	89	85	83
Buyers and Shippers, Farm Products	65	60	46	77
Buyers, Wholesale and Retail Trade	78	79	83	77
Credit Men	80	81	75	74
Funeral Directors	85	75	89	90
Health Administrators	90	91	94	95
Construction Inspectors, Public Administration	77	72	76	77
Inspectors, Except Construction; Public Administration				
Federal Public Administration and Postal Service	84	79	77	78
State Public Administration	77	69	72	60
Local Public Administration	74	68	79	88
Managers and Superintendents, Building	55	61	40	31
Office Managers (N.E.C.)	81	83	85	84
Officers, Pilots and Pursers, Ship	63	62	88	77
Officials and Administrators; Public Administrn. (N.E.C.)				
Federal Public Administration and Postal Service	92	92	93	94
State Public Administration	88	84	88	90
Local Public Administration	79	77	79	81
Officials of Lodges, Societies and Unions	86	82	89	95
Postmasters and Mail Superintendents	78	78	73	76
Purchasing Agents and Buyers (N.E.C.)	87	82	88	86
Railroad Conductors	69	68	68	77
Restaurant, Cafeteria and Bar Managers	56	63	41	34
Sales Managers and Department Heads, Retail Trade	74	76	66	53
Sales Managers, Except Retail Trade	94	92	91	93
School Administrators, College	97	97	99	99
School Administrators, Elementary and Secondary	97	97	99	99
Managers and Administrators, Salaried (N.E.C.)				
Construction	81	81	81	85
Durable Goods Manufacturing	93	92	89	89
Nondurable Goods, Incl. Not Specified Manufacturing	92	90	83	83
Transportation	85	81	88	87
Communications, Utilities and Sanitary Services	88	86	88	88
Wholesale Trade	88	86	88	84
Retail Trade				
Hardware, Farm Equipment and Building Material Retailing	82	76	79	79
General Merchandise Stores	79	78	66	54
Food Stores	70	70	51	42
Motor Vehicles and Accessories Retailing	80	74	83	89
Gasoline Service Stations	53	45	51	52
Apparel and Accessories Stores	77	81	72	69
Furniture, Home Furnishing and Equipment Stores	84	82	79	79
Other Retail Trade	79	76	71	61
Finance, Insurance and Real Estate	92	91	86	84

Business and Repair Services	89	87	92	92
Personal Services	62	71	42	32
All Other Industries	91	90	92	96
Managers and Administrators, Self-Employed (N.E.C.)				
Construction	69	67	73	77
Durable Goods, Manufacturing	72	69	43	31
Nondurable Goods, Incl. Not Specified Manufacturing	83	81	58	65
Transportation	67	65	73	75
Communications, Utilities and Sanitary Services	71	73	47	29
Wholesale Trade	78	76	72	64
Retail Trade				
Hardware, Farm Equipment and Building Material Retailing	75	73	60	46
General Merchandise Stores	60	68	48	29
Food Stores	44	44	25	12
Motor Vehicles and Accessories Retailing	75	73	50	48
Gasoline Service Stations	57	50	26	18
Apparel and Accessories Stores	74	80	67	55
Furniture, Home Furnishings and Equipment Stores	74	73	55	48
Other Retail Trade	63	66	46	34
Finance, Insurance and Real Estate	93	93	88	89
Business and Repair Services	75	71	79	79
Personal Services	53	60	44	28
All Other Industries	74	74	59	50
Managers and Administrators, Except Farm-Allocated	67	67	51	51
Sales Workers				
Advertising Agents and Salesmen	86	86	83	88
Auctioneers	69	68	31	30
Demonstrators	31	64	28	48
Hucksters and Peddlers	28	41	24	21
Insurance Agents, Brokers and Underwriters	86	82	74	76
Newsboys	12	11	20	16
Real Estate Agents and Brokers	81	84	71	84
Stock and Bond Salesmen	95	95	89	89
Salesmen and Sales Clerks (N.E.C.)				
Sales Representatives, Manufacturing Industries	88	86	49	70
Sales Representatives, Wholesale Trade	81	76	49	54
Sales Clerks, Retail Trade				
General Merchandise Stores	32	44	63	23
Food Stores	24	30	19	14
Apparel and Accessories Stores	34	37	32	25
Other Sales Clerks, Retail Trade	37	45	29	23
Salesmen, Retail Trade	65	61	37	38
Salesmen of Services and Construction	67	77	32	51
Sales Workers-Allocated	34	44	26	21
Clerical and Kindred Workers				
Bank Tellers	49	50	61	47
Billing Clerks	48	56	60	51
Bookkeepers	52	64	62	57
Cashiers	29	32	29	31

Clerical Assistants, Social Welfare	49	51	56	51
Clerical Supervisors (N.E.C.)	79	83	84	81
Collectors, Bill and Account	61	55	57	54
Counter Clerks, Except Food	37	45	38	35
Dispatchers and Starters, Vehicle	63	62	47	48
Enumerators and Interviewers	40	48	40	79
Estimators and Investigators (N.E.C.)	76	81	70	67
Expediters; Production Controllers	72	70	74	69
File Clerks	41	41	46	42
Insurance Adjusters, Examiners and Investigators	83	80	82	79
Library Attendants and Assistants	44	42	51	76
Mail Carriers, Post Office	71	64	61	73
Mail Handlers, Except Post Office	41	39	45	37
Messengers, Incl. Telegraph and Office Boys	28	23	31	31
Meter Readers, Utilities	56	46	55	50
Office Machine Operators				
Bookkeeping and Billing Machine	47	51	60	50
Calculating Machine	52	54	61	55
Computer and Peripheral Equipment	67	63	76	76
Duplicating Machine	46	42	54	46
Keypunch	49	60	65	60
Tabulating Machine	56	51	67	69
Office Machine (N.E.C.)	44	42	50	42
Payroll and Timekeeping Clerks	57	64	72	69
Postal Clerks	68	66	76	74
Proofreaders	54	70	61	61
Real Estate Appraisers	91	88	81	87
Receptionists	43	44	54	46
Secretaries	56	66	76	76
Shipping and Receiving Clerks	50	41	45	34
Statistical Clerks	59	66	71	61
Stenographers	58	81	76	75
Stock Clerks and Storekeepers	49	42	51	50
Teacher Aides, Except School Monitors	37	42	40	38
Telegraph Operators	67	64	72	71
Telephone Operators	44	49	55	52
Ticket, Station and Express Agents	74	70	88	87
Typists	46	48	56	54
Weighers	44	40	36	41
Industry				
Manufacturing	57	67	65	60
Transportation, Communications, & Other Public Utilities	61	65	76	68
Wholesale and Retail Trade	41	44	44	38
Finance, Insurance and Real Estate	51	53	61	53
Professional and Related Services	29	47	59	53
Public Administration	59	63	76	76
All Other Industries	41	51	41	39
Clerical and Kindred Workers-Allocated	39	54	41	45
Craftsmen and Kindred Workers				
Automobile Accessories Installers	43	35	47	48
Bakers	34	24	25	20

Cabinetmakers	41	30	30	25
Carpet Installers	51	41	51	48
Construction Craftsmen				
Brickmasons and Stonemasons	46	35	52	42
Bulldozer Operators	34	23	48	49
Carpenters	42	33	51	56
Cement and Concrete Finishers	32	21	47	57
Electricians	70	66	64	64
Excavating, Grading and Road Machine Operators, Except Bulldozers	41	30	48	45
Floor Layers, Except Tile Setters	48	41	51	57
Painters, Construction and Maintenance	32	18	40	46
Paperhangers	39	28	17	57
Plasterers	42	33	64	57
Plumbers and Pipe Fitters	62	57	65	64
Roofers and Slaters	32	18	42	57
Structural Metal Craftsmen	61	58	59	53
Tile Setters	50	42	43	57
Cranemen, Derrickmen and Hoistmen	46	39	57	55
Decorators and Window Dressers	46	53	45	36
Dental Laboratory Technicians	61	60	57	47
Electric Power Linemen and Cablemen	70	66	63	64
Engravers, Except Photoengravers	50	46	45	47
Foremen (N.E.C.)				
Construction	62	60	61	60
Manufacturing				
Metal Industries	71	70	64	61
Machinery, Except Electrical	76	75	76	71
Electrical Machinery, Equipment and Supplies	78	78	64	58
Transportation Equipment	77	77	76	72
Other Durable Goods	65	65	60	56
Food and Kindred Products	63	61	42	50
Textiles, Textile Products and Apparel	48	50	46	31
Other Nondurable Goods, Incl. Not Specified Manufacturing	72	78	62	57
Transportation	67	66	67	62
Communications, Utilities and Sanitary Services	77	76	85	84
Wholesale and Retail Trade	67	65	64	51
All Other Industries	66	65	72	61
Furniture and Wood Finishers	30	22	29	14
Furriers	46	44	23	48
Glaziers	56	50	43	48
Inspectors, Scalers and Graders; Log and Lumber	36	26	28	19
Inspectors (N.E.C.)	66	61	37	36
Jewelers and Watchmakers	53	49	39	29
Locomotive Engineers	69	69	69	48
Locomotive Firemen	72	69	47	48
Mechanics and Repairmen				
Air Conditioning, Heating and Refrigeration	61	54	65	64
Aircraft	72	68	65	64
Automobile Body Repairmen	47	37	50	51
Automobile Mechanics	45	36	55	54

Data Processing Machine Repairmen	85	78	76	73
Farm Implement	44	33	60	58
Heavy Equipment Mechanics, Including Diesel	57	50	59	57
Household Appliance and Accessory Installers and Mechanics	58	50	46	56
Loom Fixers	30	18	60	58
Office Machine	69	61	74	65
Radio and Television	60	56	54	59
Railroad and Car Shop	50	43	66	58
Miscellaneous Mechanics and Repairmen	60	53	60	58
Mechanics, Except Auto, Apprentices	58	52	62	58
Not Specified Mechanics and Repairmen	56	51	54	44
Metal Craftsmen, Except Mechanics				
Blacksmiths	37	26	52	56
Boilermakers	56	51	68	56
Forgemen and Hammermen	48	42	47	39
Heat Treaters, Annealers and Temperers	53	47	58	56
Job and Die Setters, Metal	54	50	56	51
Machinists	62	57	48	55
Millwrights	62	60	63	64
Molders, Metal	38	30	39	28
Pattern and Model Makers, Except Paper	72	70	65	61
Rollers and Finishers, Metal	52	47	48	41
Sheetmetal Workers and Tinsmiths	63	59	57	62
Shipfitters	58	52	52	56
Tool and Die Makers	73	70	64	64
Millers; Grain, Flour and Food	27	14	47	48
Motion Picture Projectionists	50	39	48	48
Opticians and Lens Grinders and Polishers	61	62	48	37
Piano and Organ Tuners and Repairmen	54	44	47	48
Power Station Operators	75	71	71	75
Printing Craftsmen				
Bookbinders	40	52	37	29
Compositors and Typesetters	64	61	48	45
Electrotypers and Stereotypers	68	65	45	42
Photoengravers and Lithographers	75	73	59	52
Pressmen and Plate Printers, Printing	63	60	48	46
Shoe Repairmen	18	11	27	12
Sign Painters and Letterers	48	39	30	36
Stationary Engineers	64	60	63	61
Stone Cutters and Stone Carvers	33	20	23	48
Tailors	28	22	28	19
Telephone Installers and Repairmen	74	68	76	65
Telephone Linemen and Splicers	69	60	70	40
Upholsterers	33	22	29	19
Craftsmen and Kindred Workers (N.E.C.)	49	45	36	29
Former Members of the Armed Forces	42	38	36	48
Craftsmen and Kindred Workers-Allocated	44	36	28	22
Operatives, Except Transport				
Asbestos and Insulation Workers	61	58	44	22
Assemblers	41	41	42	33
Blasters and Powdermen	36	26	31	22

Bottling and Canning Operatives	22	26	18	23
Chainmen, Rodmen and Axmen; Surveying	44	35	31	22
Checkers, Examiners and Inspectors; Manufacturing	47	42	41	32
Clothing Ironers and Pressers	11	12	19	08
Cutting Operatives (N.E.C.)	33	28	28	17
Dressmakers and Seamstresses, Except Factory	18	12	23	18
Drillers, Earth	44	36	38	35
Dry Wall Installers and Lathers	51	45	46	22
Dyers	29	16	33	26
Garage Workers and Gas Station Attendants	20	19	16	12
Graders and Sorters, Manufacturing	17	20	23	18
Produce Graders and Packers, Except Factory and Farm	05	04	10	05
Laundry and Drycleaning Operatives (N.E.C.)	14	15	18	07
Meat Cutters and Butchers, Except Manufacturing	54	47	26	25
Meat Cutters and Butchers, Manufacturing	33	31	20	14
Meat Wrappers, Retail Trade	29	20	40	43
Metalworking Operatives, Except Precision Machine				
Filers, Polishers, Sanders and Buffers	30	19	30	23
Furnacemen, Smeltermen, and Pourers	43	35	50	49
Heaters, Metal	49	42	39	30
Metal Platers	45	37	43	34
Punch and Stamping Press Operatives	40	37	40	30
Riveters and Fasteners	28	26	33	23
Solderers	29	26	41	31
Welders and Flame Cutters	49	41	45	40
Milliners	19	27	26	20
Mine Operatives (N.E.C.)				
Coal Mining	35	25	47	39
Crude Petroleum and Natural Gas Extraction	48	41	34	25
Mining and Quarrying, Except Fuel	42	31	54	39
Mixing Operatives	43	33	35	35
Oilers and Greasers, Except Auto	41	31	40	44
Packers and Wrappers, Except Meat and Produce	24	25	31	23
Painters, Manufactured Articles	36	25	34	22
Photographic Process Workers	51	53	47	42
Precision Machine Operatives				
Drill Press Operatives	42	39	42	38
Grinding Machine Operatives	52	47	53	49
Lathe and Milling Machine Operatives	59	53	51	50
Precision Machine Operatives (N.E.C.)	56	53	37	34
Sailors and Deckhands	36	23	43	22
Sawyers	19	08	30	19
Sewers and Stitchers	14	11	26	13
Shoemaking Machine Operatives	15	08	28	16
Stationary Firemen	45	38	30	20
Textile Operatives				
Carding, Lapping and Combing Operatives	17	07	31	18
Knitters, Loopers and Toppers	19	17	28	18
Spinners, Twisters and Winders	16	09	26	18
Weavers	22	12	38	26
Textile Operatives (N.E.C.)	19	11	29	17
Winding Operatives (N.E.C.)	42	50	40	28

Industry				
Manufacturing-Durable Goods				
Lumber and Wood Products, Except Furniture	19	10	26	14
Furniture and Fixtures	17	10	26	16
Stone, Clay and Glass Products				
Glass and Glass Products	44	42	38	37
Cement, Concrete, Gypsum and Plaster Products	31	17	24	27
Other Stone, Clay and Glass Products	32	21	33	23
Primary Metal Industries				
Blast Furnaces, Steel Works and Rolling and Finishing Mills	51	44	56	51
Other Primary Iron and Steel Industries	37	27	40	28
Primary Nonferrous Industries	45	39	40	39
Fabricated Metal Industries, Including Not Specific Metal				
Cutlery, Hand tools and Other Hardware	32	26	41	33
Fabricated Structural Metal Products	34	23	30	18
Screw Machine Products and Metal Stamping	32	26	35	32
Miscellaneous Fabricated Metal Products and Not Specified Metal	39	33	33	26
Machinery, Except Electrical				
Farm Machinery and Equipment	44	37	38	42
Construction and Material Handling Machines	57	51	54	42
Metalworking Machinery	54	52	41	39
Office and Accounting Machines and Electronic Computing Equipment	50	54	50	46
Other Machinery, Except Electrical	47	43	44	41
Electrical Machinery, Equipment and Supplies				
Household Appliances	41	37	35	29
Radio, T.V. and Communication Equipment	46	52	56	47
Electrical Machinery, Equipment and Supplies (N.E.C.)	40	40	42	32
Not Specified Electrical Machinery, Equipment and Supplies	40	45	41	29
Transportation Equipment				
Motor Vehicles and Motor Vehicle Equipment	52	49	56	56
Aircraft and Parts	58	53	60	57
Other Transportation Equipment	38	29	33	22
Professional and Photographic Equipment and Watches	43	50	38	27
Ordnance	46	70	57	49
Miscellaneous Manufacturing Industries	22	21	29	19
Durable Goods-Allocated	36	32	33	25
Manufacturing-Nondurable Goods				
Food and Kindred Products				
Meat Products	19	20	19	13
Dairy Products	46	38	29	29
Canning and Preserving Fruits, Vegetables, and Seafoods	09	08	11	12
Bakery Products	31	24	37	30
Beverage Industries	45	41	39	35
Other Food and Kindred Products	30	21	30	23
Tobacco Manufacturers	20	18	25	17
Apparel and Other Fabricated Textile Products				

Apparel and Accessories	15	12	25	12
Miscellaneous Fabricated Textile Products	16	09	24	10
Paper and Allied Products				
Pulp, Paper and Paperboard Mills	56	52	51	48
Miscellaneous Fabricated Textile Products	38	40	36	24
Paperboard Containers and Boxes	33	27	31	23
Printing, Publishing and Allied Industries	41	44	37	29
Chemicals and Allied Products				
Industrial Chemicals	65	60	62	62
Synthetic Fibers	49	43	56	54
Soaps and Cosmetics	41	49	40	38
Other Chemicals and Allied Products	57	54	62	41
Petroleum and Coal Products	68	65	62	21
Rubber and Miscellaneous Plastic Products				
Rubber Products	48	48	44	35
Miscellaneous Plastic Products	29	32	33	24
Leather and Leather Products				
Tanned, Curried and Finished Leather	24	14	27	17
Footwear, Except Rubber	17	11	27	17
Leather Products, Except Footwear	15	14	25	10
Nondurable Goods-Allocated	24	25	26	16
Not Specified Manufacturing Industries	26	24	28	25
Nonmanufacturing Industries				
Construction	32	30	28	44
Railroads and Railway Express Service	32	19	25	22
Transportation, Except Railroads	57	52	27	45
Communications, Utilities and Sanitary Services	56	50	66	62
Wholesale Trade	24	20	20	20
Retail Trade	24	20	24	16
Business and Repair Services	37	29	31	31
Public Administration	51	45	51	57
All Other Industries	28	24	28	20
Operatives, Except Transport-Allocated	22	16	16	15
Transport Equipment Operatives				
Boatmen and Canalmen	37	27	25	42
Bus Drivers	40	36	24	28
Conductors and Motormen, Urban Rail Transit	63	60	29	42
Deliverymen and Routemen	48	38	31	37
Fork Lift and Tow Motor Operatives	38	27	55	50
Motormen; Mine, Factor, Logging Camp, etc.	37	28	29	42
Parking Attendants	25	18	28	42
Railroad Brakemen	65	61	59	42
Railroad Switchmen	65	60	70	64
Taxicab Drivers and Chauffeurs	35	26	29	21
Truck Drivers	41	31	51	51
Transport Equipment Operatives-Allocated	34	21	26	24
Laborers, Except Farm				
Animal Caretakers, Except Farm	25	20	25	23
Carpenters' Helpers	14	06	22	20
Construction Laborers, Except Carpenters' Helpers	24	13	28	42
Fishermen and Oystermen	16	07	06	20

Freight and Material Handlers	35	25	34	26
Garbage Collectors	22	08	25	34
Gardeners and Groundkeepers, Except Farm	14	06	12	17
Longshoremen and Stevedores	40	29	53	20
Lumbermen, Raftsmen and Woodchoppers	12	04	16	11
Stock Handlers	19	19	26	22
Teamsters	19	08	24	20
Vehicle Washers and Equipment Cleaners	15	10	18	16
Warehousemen (N.E.C.)	49	40	52	47
Industry				
Manufacturing				
Durable Goods				
Lumber and Wood Products, Except Furniture	13	05	16	13
Furniture and Fixtures	14	05	23	19
Stone, Clay and Glass Products				
Cement, Concrete, Gypsum and Plaster Products	28	16	34	25
Structural Clay Products	17	06	34	25
Other Stone, Clay and Glass Products	35	25	35	24
Primary Metal Industries				
Blast Furnaces, Steel Works and Rolling and Finishing Mills	43	28	54	45
Other Primary Iron and Steel Industries	30	20	42	45
Primary Nonferrous Industries	40	28	48	45
Fabricated Metal Industries, Including Not Specified Metal	24	17	27	15
Machinery, Except Electrical	38	28	29	45
Electrical Machinery, Equipment and Supplies	32	27	42	32
Transportation Equipment				
Major Vehicles and Motor Vehicle Equipment	40	29	59	41
Ship and Boat Building and Repairing	29	18	39	41
Other Transportation Equipment	32	21	32	41
Professional and Photographic Equipment and Watches	28	25	33	24
Ordnance	37	21	56	49
Miscellaneous Manufacturing Industries	13	06	21	14
Manufacturing, Durable Goods-Allocated	15	07	32	*
Nondurable Goods				
Food and Kindred Products				
Meat Products	23	16	16	17
Dairy Products	34	33	16	14
Canning and Preserving Fruits, Vegetables and Seafoods	10	05	12	14
Grain-Mill Products	26	13	16	14
Beverage Industries	27	14	16	14
Other Foods and Kindred Products	16	06	21	14
Tobacco Manufacturers	11	05	07	16
Textile Mill Products				
Yarn, Thread and Fabric Mills	13	05	19	12
Other Textile Mill Products	15	06	26	13
Apparel and Other Fabricated Textile Products	14	08	23	14
Paper and Allied Products				
Pulp, Paper and Paperboard Mills	49	38	23	35
Other Paper and Allied Products	25	18	30	35

*No cases

Printing, Publishing and Allied Products	18	18	23	16
Chemicals and Allied Products	40	31	32	35
Petroleum and Coal Products	48	36	22	16
Rubber and Miscellaneous Plastic Products	35	29	30	25
Leather and Leather Products	14	06	22	10
Nondurable Goods-Allocated	09	03	22	16
Not Specified Manufacturing Industries	21	12	27	21
Nonmanufacturing Industries				
Railroads and Railway Express Service	26	13	29	32
Transportation, Except Railroads	28	17	31	54
Communications, Utilities and Sanitary Services	25	13	26	13
Transportation, Communications, Utilities and Sanitary Services-Allocated	07	03	13	*
Wholesale Trade	14	07	11	13
Retail Trade	10	08	11	14
Business and Repair Services	20	14	14	18
Personal Services	03	02	04	04
Public Administration	19	07	22	23
All Other Industries	13	08	17	10
Laborers, Except Farm-Allocated	15	07	12	11
Farmers and Farm Managers				
Farmers, Owners and Tenants	31	19	13	13
Farm Managers	52	43	35	29
Farmers and Farm Managers-Allocated	18	09	20	16
Farm Laborers and Farm Foremen				
Farm Foremen	34	22	41	64
Farm Laborers, Wage Workers	04	02	03	03
Farm Laborers, Unpaid Family Workers	15	13	17	15
Farm Service Laborers, Self-Employed	37	30	23	08
Farm Laborers and Farm Formen-Allocated	02	01	03	01
Service Workers, Except Private Household				
Cleaning Service Workers				
Chambermaids and Maids, Except Private Household	05	14	10	03
Cleaners and Charwomen	09	07	14	06
Janitors and Sextons	19	10	16	14
Food Service Workers				
Bartenders	42	36	29	22
Busboys	12	13	11	09
Cooks, Except Private Household	14	18	16	08
Dishwashers	07	09	06	02
Food Counter and Fountain Workers	17	17	16	12
Waiters	19	24	18	13
Food Service Workers (N.E.C.)	15	16	16	12
Health Service Workers				
Dental Assistants	41	40	51	49
Health Aides. Except Nursing	38	34	46	34
Health Trainees	42	35	43	45
Lay Midwives	34	20	37	28
Nursing Aides, Orderlies and Attendants	28	32	31	23

*No cases

Practical Nurses	44	43	55	46
Personal Service Workers				
Airline Stewardesses	69	68	90	89
Attendants, Recreation and Amusement	24	25	22	37
Attendants, Personal Service (N.E.C.)	31	27	32	31
Baggage Porters and Bellhops	30	24	38	31
Barbers	40	31	37	34
Boarding and Lodging Housekeepers	25	33	27	20
Bootblacks	02	00	37	31
Child Care Workers, Except Private Household	23	32	20	18
Elevator Operators	21	12	25	14
Hairdressers and Cosmetologists	35	46	40	34
Housekeepers, Except Private Household	36	48	36	28
School Monitors	30	40	27	44
Ushers, Recreation and Amusement	15	16	18	31
Welfare Service Aides	38	47	38	32
Protective Service Workers				
Crossing Guards and Bridge Tenders	18	07	21	15
Firemen, Fire Protection	74	69	76	72
Guards and Watchmen	43	32	42	47
Marshals and Constables	60	52	34	64
Policemen and Detectives				
Public	77	71	74	84
Private	59	54	47	54
Sheriffs and Bailiffs	65	58	72	77
Service Workers, Except Private Household-Allocated	15	11	16	12
Private Household Workers				
Child Care Workers, Private Household	10	10	09	03
Cooks, Private Household	02	06	06	01
Housekeepers, Private Household	03	06	05	02
Laundresses, Private Household	00	06	01	00
Maids and Servants, Private Household	02	02	03	01
Private Household Workers-Allocated	01	05	02	00

***Source**: Charles B. Nam, John LaRocque, Mary G. Powers, and Joan Holmberg, "Occupational Status Scores: Stability and Change," *Proceedings of the American Statistical Association, Social Statistics Section* (Washington, D.C.: American Statistical Association, 1975), pp. 572-575.

**N.E.C.=Not Elsewhere Classified

Table B1.
Scores for Categories of Years of School Completed: 1980

Category:	*Score:*
College: 4 years of more	92
College: 1 to 3 years	76
High school: 4 years	50
High school: 1 to 3 years	25
Elementary School: 8 years	13
Elementary School: 5 to 7 years	06
Elementary School: 0 to 4 years	02

Source: U.S. Bureau of the Census, *Statistical Abstract of the United States, 1981* (Washington, DC: U.S. Government Printing Office, 1981),p.142.

Table B2.
Scores for Household Income: 1979

Category:	*Score:*
$50,000 or more	98
$35,000 to 49,999	93
$25,000 to 34,999	81
$20,000 to 24,999	67
$15,000 to 19,999	54
$10,000 to 14,999	38
$5,000 to 9,999	21
Under $5,000	07

Source: U.S. Bureau of the Census, *Statistical Abstract of the United States, 1981* (Washington, DC: U.S. Government Printing Office, 1981),p.432.

INDEX

ABOUT THE AUTHORS

CHARLES B. NAM, Ph.D., is current Professor of Sociology and Research Associate of the Center for the Study of Population at Florida State University, and the author of numerous publications on demography, social stratification and related topics. He was on the staff of the U.S. Bureau of the Census earlier in his career.

MARY G. POWERS, Ph.D., is currently Professor in the Department of Sociology and Anthropology, Fordham University, and has many publications and reports on demography, social stratification, and urban sociological subjects. She also served with the U.S. Bureau of the Census, and more recently was chair of its Population Advisory Committee.